Attachment of the Young
Imprinting and Other Developments

CONTEMPORARY
SCIENCE
PAPERBACKS
38

F. V. SMITH
Professor of Psychology, University of Durham

Attachment of the Young

Imprinting and Other Developments

OLIVER & BOYD *Edinburgh*

156.315
Sm5a
74180
April, 1971

OLIVER AND BOYD LTD
Tweeddale Court Edinburgh 1

First published 1969
© 1969 F. V. Smith

05 001744 6

Set in Times New Roman and printed in
Great Britain by Richard Clay (The Chaucer Press) Ltd
Bungay, Suffolk

Preface

Within the last few decades, the scientific study of animal behaviour has revealed many innate reactions in a wide range of species. These are not only interesting in themselves, but help us to understand more clearly the problems of adjustment to different environments with different innate resources. In this process of adjustment the importance of early experience has been repeatedly demonstrated, and perhaps most dramatically in phenomena of the type known as imprinting.

The present short work attempts to provide the readers with an introduction to the literature on early attachment and some of the implications which arise from it for other fields of study. The bibliography should enable interested persons to proceed further.

My thanks are due to Dr J. D. Delius for the preparation of Fig. 1, to Mr Malcolm Rolling and Mr K. Nott for help in the preparation of other diagrams and to Dr R. J. Wootton and Mr Denis Parker for help with the proofs.

Grateful acknowledgement is here made to Dr Gilbert Gottlieb for permission to use Plates I, IIa and IIb and to Drs H. Moltz and L. J. Stettner for the use of Fig. 4. Plates I and IIa and Fig. 4 appeared in the *Journal of Comparative and Physiological Psychology*, Plate IIb in the *Natural History Magazine*, for which due acknowledgement is made to the Editors. Plate V appeared in *Psychobiology*, published by W. H. Freeman & Co. of San Francisco; due acknowledgement is made to the Company and the photographer, Mr Gordon Coster of Chicago, Illinois, for permission to use this illustration.

F. V. SMITH

Contents

1. Introduction

The term 'imprinting' – from the German verb *prägen* = to coin or stamp and the related noun, *Die Prägung* = stamping – appears to have been used for the first time by Oskar Heinroth (1911) in relation to his experiments with birds, chiefly the large family of waterfowl (Anatidae). Certain members of this family, in particular newly hatched geese and ducks, were seen to respond to the first large moving object they encountered in much the same way as they normally react to their parents. Human attendants, for example, were followed consistently and in some cases in later years became the object of sexual advances by the birds.

The phenomenon is most readily observed in precocial species, i.e. those in which the young are capable of locomotion at birth or soon afterwards; among birds, this usually means that the young are nidifugous, i.e. like domestic chickens, they leave the nest soon after birth. Experimental evidence will be considered, however, of some early moulding of the attention of altricial birds, i.e. those which are helpless when hatched and in consequence tend to be nidicolous, i.e. stay in the nest for some time.

While the term 'imprinting' must be associated with the work of Heinroth and the considerable extension of his insight by Konrad Lorenz, the actual phenomenon has been known for a long time. As will be shown, Aristotle writing in the fourth century B.C. was clearly aware of some of its aspects. Pliny, the Roman encyclopaedist (*Natural History*, Book X. 51), after referring to the vigilance of the geese which gave warning of an attack on the Capitol, mentions a goose which, it is said, was the constant companion of the philosopher Lacydes, 'never leaving him, not in public, in the baths, nor by day or night'. Watt (1951) records that Reginald, a medieval monk of Durham, in 1167 recorded instances of young eider ducks following human beings. The birds are known to have nested on the Farne Islands off the north-east coast of England for centuries, as they do today. St Cuthbert, who died on the islands in 687, had noted their habits and breeding seasons and had given them special protection.

Douglas Spalding, an Englishman who died in his late thirties in 1877, made several important discoveries. He is known (see Haldane, 1954) to have worked as a slater in Aberdeen, where he attended the lectures of Professor Alexander Bain. For a time Spalding served as tutor to the two sons of Lord Amberley, one of whom is better known today as Bertrand (Earl) Russell. Actually, he appears to have been mainly concerned with Bertrand's elder brother; but both Lord and Lady Amberley were interested in Spalding's work and co-operated with him in some of his experiments. In 1872 he read a paper before the British Association and attracted the attention of John Stuart Mill; a year later, the paper was published in *Macmillan's Magazine*. Spalding had noted that as soon as domestic chicks were able to walk about they would approach and follow objects moving across his table. He also recorded that chicks fitted with small hoods which deprived them of visual experience, would follow his hand when the hoods were removed at the age of three days. There was a brief period in which the chick remained motionless, emitting high-pitched 'fear' chirps, but very soon the chicks were following his hand consistently. Those unhooded on the fourth day, however, fled from the experimenter, displaying every sign of fear. Spalding concluded that this reversal of the chicks' behaviour could not have been due directly to experience, but to changes occurring within the chick. He had not only made important observations on the responses of approach and attachment in young birds, but had indicated two associated problems: namely, the operation of a 'critical period' during which following responses are most likely to occur, and the possibility of changes within the chick which determine the emergence of fear and possibly contribute thereby to the termination of the 'critical period'.

The foregoing introduction will have indicated the nature of the phenomenon known as 'imprinting', which to date has been studied mainly in birds. It should be pointed out, however, that analogous and not necessarily identical phenomena have been observed in other species, including bees, cichlid fish, and mammals such as sheep and goats, where auditory and olfactory impressions are important, and in chimpanzees, where tactile cues seem to predominate. Here again, there is evidence that the type of attachment achieved in early life, and indeed the failure to achieve an attachment, may have important consequences for the subsequent normality of the individual. The studies with bees, fish and birds are of intense biological interest, and despite the differences in evolutionary development represented by these different species, it is natural that many people concerned with delinquency and the impaired emotional and intellectual development of children should look to studies with other species, particularly mammalian species, for possible cues for insight and research.

If the reader will now consult the Contents, the sequence of the treatment hereafter will become clear.

2. Brief Review of the Historical Background to the Study of Imprinting

Haldane (1954), in a brief note to a reprinting of Spalding's paper of 1873, writes, 'Had he lived even to the age of fifty, there can be little doubt that he would be recognised as the principal founder of what is now called Ethology.' This is a defensible statement, for Spalding not only devised a number of interesting experiments and useful techniques, but was active in discussions of the related philosophical issues. Romanes in *Mental Evolution in Animals* (1883) made reference to his work; so, too, did William James in his *Principles of Psychology* (1890) in the chapter on instinct, and Drever in his *Instinct in Man* as late as 1921. But references to Spalding were very few in the first half of the twentieth century, when a new emphasis in the scientific study of behaviour became apparent in Europe – one which has become associated with the names of Oskar Heinroth, Konrad Lorenz, Niko Tinbergen and their many co-workers. This approach to the study of behaviour has become known as Ethology of which, it should be emphasised, the study of imprinting forms only a part.

The distinctive feature of the ethological approach to behaviour is the emphasis upon evolution as applied not only to structural or morphological characteristics of animals, but especially to patterns of behaviour. In the immense volume of empirical data assembled in Aristotle's *De Anima*, *Historia Animalium* and *De Generatione Animalium*, in the forty-four volumes of Buffon's *Histoire Naturelle* published between 1749 and 1804, and in Lamarck's *Philosophie Zoologique* (1809) many observations of behaviour occur; but Charles

4

Robert Darwin, after the publication in 1859 of his epoch-making work *On the Origin of the Species*, specifically extended his fundamental thesis of modification of the species by natural selection to consider actual behaviour. In *The Descent of Man* (1871) Darwin drew attention to features of similarity between human reasoning and similar processes in higher animals. *The Expression of Emotions in Animals and Man* (1872) offered an evolutionary interpretation of characteristic facial and postural changes during strong emotion. In the delineation of patterns of behaviour and in suggesting a possible continuity of a human grimace with a comparable gesture in dogs and apes or that such a behavioural feature may be inherited from a common ancestor, there is definitely an ethological trend.

The influence of the concept of evolution by natural selection was widespread. In 1869 Francis Galton, Darwin's half-cousin, published *Studies of Hereditary Genius*, applying the principles of variation, selection and adaptation to the study of human performance and racial groups. Lloyd Morgan's *Introduction to Comparative Psychology* (1894) and *Animal Behaviour* (1900) revealed an evolutionary approach; but the most influential writings in this respect were those of Wm McDougall. In 1908 he published his *Introduction to Social Psychology*. When he died in 1938, in Durham, North Carolina, the book was already in its twenty-third edition and many more have followed. The persistent emphasis of the work was upon an evolutionary continuity in behaviour between man and animals by means of McDougall's particular form of vitalism ('wherever there is life, there is mind') and the basic concept of instinct. An instinct was defined as 'an inherited or innate psycho-physical disposition which determines its possessor to perceive or pay attention to objects of a certain class, and to experience an emotional excitement of a particular quality upon perceiving such an object and to act in regard to it in a particular manner, or, at least, to experience an impulse to such action'. Man and the higher animals were endowed by assumption with a number of relatively distinct instincts, each mediated by a separate neurological correlate. In a later work,

An Outline of Psychology, he illustrated the action of a stimulus impinging upon the instinct by the analogy of a specific key which fits and activates the innate lock or instinct. The broad correspondence with the theory of specific stimuli or 'releasers' which activate an Innate Releasing Mechanism, as developed by Lorenz and Tinbergen, will be apparent.

Up to the time of his death in 1938 there was no convincing evidence in support of McDougall's hypothesis of specific neurological correlates underlying the separate instincts. Indeed, support for his position seemed to be fading. Lashley, in his monograph *Brain Mechanisms and Intelligence*, had shown by surgical removal of different amounts of the cortex, the uppermost layer of the brain, that the ability of rats to learn maze patterns was roughly proportional to the total weight of cortical tissue remaining, irrespective of the place from which it was removed. These findings he summarised in the two principles of *Mass Action* and *Equipotentiality*, and the initial implication was obviously not very favourable to an hypothesis based upon specificity of neurological correlates. Again, McDougall's claim, supported by experiments with successive generations of rats, that instincts were specific habits of reaction acquired by experience and passed on and perfected in successive generations, had not been confirmed by the more rigorous experiments of Agar *et al.* (1935–54) and Crew (1936). But it was still possible that specific patterns of behaviour and emotional activity could be mediated by regions of the brain below the cortex, and this is what later discoveries definitely tended to show.

In a series of papers appearing in 1943 and 1944, W. R. Hess and M. Brügger described how they had introduced very fine electrodes into different areas in the hypothalamus of normal, intact cats and by passing very small electric currents were able to elicit such behaviour as fighting, sleeping and eating. The behaviour appeared to be normal in the sense that it was co-ordinated and apparently purposeful. The cats not only went to sleep, but also searched for a place in which to sleep. The hypothalamus is a relatively small part of the mammalian brain but from its central position it has, directly or indirectly, a wealth of functional connections with other parts of the brain. Since the early papers of Hess and Brügger, centres have been found in the hypothalamus which influence sexual activity in addition to sleeping, fighting and eating. Anderson and McCann (1955) have shown, for example, that goats already satiated with water can be induced to drink excessively if a certain area of the hypothalamus is stimulated either electrically or by direct application of a weak saline solution. Fisher (1964) and others have carried further the technique of direct application of solutions and hormones to the hypothalamus and adjoining areas and seem well on the way to isolating a circuit which, when activated, could reverberate for a time, suppressing other drives and thus ensure that the needs of the animal for water were satisfied. The notion of different 'neurological correlates' mediating specific types of purposeful behaviour, which had no more than hypothetical status in McDougall's day, is now on much surer ground.

Further support for the existence of innate patterns of behaviour came from the work of two other men using the different but basically simple method of observing long and carefully the behaviour of closely related species. C. O. Whitman, a professor of Zoology at Harvard University, was mainly concerned with the fine gradations produced by evolution in pigeons. His observations, supported by the beautiful coloured illustrations of his Japanese artists, are recorded in the several volumes of his *Orthogenic Evolution in Pigeons* (1919). In a lecture delivered in 1898, he stated: 'Instincts and organs are to be studied from the common standpoint of phyletic descent.' Repeated observation had convinced Whitman that endogenous movements – facets of behaviour which came from within the bird – were sufficiently consistent within related species to form a basis of classification. Independently, Oskar Heinroth, a curator at the Berlin Zoo for many years, had come to a similar conclusion from his close observation of geese and ducks.

In Heinroth's now famous paper to the Fifth Ornithological Congress in Berlin in 1910, on the 'Ethology and Psychology

of the Anatidae', the concept of homology emerges. According to Lorenz (1955), homology simply means 'inherited from
a common ancestor'. What Whitman and Heinroth, who began
by studying morphological or bodily characteristics, had done
was to discover a whole range of behaviour patterns which in
the view of ethologists vary from species to species and from
genus to genus, just as reliably as morphological characteristics; or, as Lorenz has claimed (1955), 'there are behaviour
patterns, whose geological age is obviously as great as that of
the most conservative bodily characteristics,' and later, 'the
comparative method to which we owe all or most of our
knowledge concerning the evolutionary history of living
creatures is just as applicable to these behaviour patterns as
to any organs.'

An example offered by Lorenz (1966) is that of the head-
scratching movement common to most reptiles, birds and
mammals, the embryos of which develop within an amniotic
sac. In the European Bullfinch (*Pyrrhula pyrrhula*) the claw
(hind foot) scratches the side of the head, over and outside
the lowered wing, just as the dog scratches the side of the head
with the hind foot, over the front shoulder. Clumsy perhaps,
but as Lorenz remarks, 'Before the bird can scratch, it must
reconstruct the old spatial relationship of the limbs of the
four-legged common ancestor.'

As the studies of W. R. Hess indicated, the activation of a
pattern of activity by the electrode in the hypothalamus of the
cat produced not only specific behaviour, such as sleep, to take
one example, but also appetitive behaviour. The cat not only
went to sleep, but first searched for a suitable place. Much
animal behaviour, as Whitman's student, Wallace Craig (1918),
pointed out, consists in searching for the appropriate stimulus
which allows a releasing or consummatory act to take place,
and the ultimate survival value of the activity and the goal for
which the animal is striving are frequently different.

The recourse to the experimental study of behaviour has
been a marked feature of the ethological movement, though
it should be noted that much admirable work by Kuo, Thorn-
dike, Lashley and his student, F. A. Beach, was done in

America, without the direct stimulus of European workers. Lashley's important paper on 'Experimental analysis of instinctive behaviour' (1938) was an indication of what had been achieved and what was to come with greater awareness by American and European experimentalists of each other's work. The number of specific reaction patterns discovered is enormous. Some are reported in Tinbergen's *The Study of Instinct* (1951). A few are described here.

Brückner (1933) demonstrated that a domestic hen would fail to come to the rescue of her chick struggling under a glass bell. When the bell was raised a little, permitting the chick's distress chirps to be heard, the hen responded immediately. Tinbergen (1951) has shown that male, Three-spined Sticklebacks (*Gasterosteus aculeatus*), which in the breeding season develop a more intense red underside and engage in a great deal of fighting with other males in the maintenance of territories, will attack a variety of crude plaster models of fish, varying in shape, especially if the model has a red underside. In feeding, the chick of the Herring Gull (*Larus argentatus*) pecks at a red spot on the lower mandible of the yellow bill of the mother who regurgitates food on to the ground, picks it up in the tips of the beak and presents it to the young. Experiments with models of a bird's head by Tinbergen have shown that while spots of a variety of colours and shades on the bill will evoke responses, red spots are most effective.

The ethological approach has been severely criticised, notably by Lehrman (1953), on the grounds that apparent homologies may be misleading. Similar behaviour in different species may not be mediated by similar mechanisms, and a convergence of mechanisms or outcomes in evolution could also result in a false homology. Again, Lehrman was disturbed by the apparent readiness of ethologists to abstract aspects of behaviour and then 'reify' them as specific, autonomous mechanisms. However, it should be noted that evidence has been accumulating over the years which can give an answer at least to some of Lehrman's misgivings. Much of this evidence is summarised in a paper by von Holst and Ursula von St Paul (1963).

W. R. Hess, in addition to his work on stimulation of the hypothalamus, had inserted fine electrodes into an even lower area, the brain stem, and had been able, in the presence of an appropriate object, to stimulate cats to eat, attack or flee, by passing small electric currents to the implanted electrodes. If the current was sufficiently strong, the animal could be made to chew inedible objects and attack a friendly human observer. This work was extended by von Holst and von St Paul. By appropriate stimulation in the hypothalamus, lower parts of the thalamus, the paleostriatum and anterior parts of the mid brain (see Fig. 1), they succeeded in eliciting from domestic fowls a wide range of activities including sitting, preening, scratching with the feet, and more complex sequences such as seeking and eating food and drinking water. The most interesting aspect of their work is associated with the operation of the so-called 'drives' where the contribution of the external, perceptual situation *and* the internal drive state, activated by electrical stimulation, are apparent. In one series of experiments, a rooster fitted with electrodes was induced to attack a stuffed Pole-cat which at first it scarcely appeared to notice. As the electrical stimulation was applied, however, the behaviour of the bird changed to one of marked alertness, visual fixation of the Pole-cat, deliberate approach and finally a full attack with spurs forward. So, too, after sustained stimulation, the bird was induced to fly up and attack a friendly keeper's face. Apparently, the perceptual cues do contribute to the behaviour. If the room is bare of perceivable objects, the rooster, under electrical stimulation, exhibits only a marked restlessness.

Lorenz could well feel a genuine satisfaction at the Tenth International Ethological Conference in Stockholm in 1967. The whole of the proceedings were marked by great cordiality not least that between Lehrman and Lorenz, and the range of the studies was vast. His latest book, *On Aggression* (1966), deals with the remarkable blend of instinct and ritualisation which ensures that animals normally do not destroy other members of their own species, whereas man, albeit with greater intelligence, has not the same safeguards.

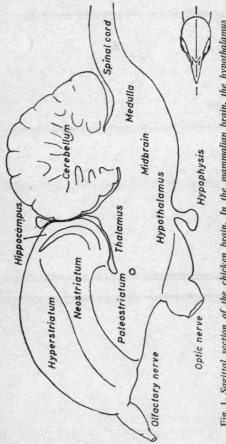

Fig. 1. Sagittal section of the chicken brain. In the mammalian brain, the hypothalamus occupies a more central position.

EARLY STUDIES OF IMPRINTING

The early studies of Spalding (1873) have been noted, and while these were experimental studies it would no doubt be possible to find many observations of imprinting scattered throughout general literature. Mills (1896) cites a letter from T. Mann Jones which describes the attachment of two small broods of chickens to a large tom-cat in whose fur they nestled when cold and slept at night. When half-grown, they would run towards any cat or its mewing and would have been killed but for the vigilance of their protector. They took refuge with the cat when a broody hen clucked or cocks crowed. J. B. Watson (1908), better known later as the protagonist of behaviourism, reported his experiences with terns on the Tortugas Islands. He reared eight Sooty Tern (*Sterna fuscata*) and three Noddy Tern (*Anoüs stolidus*) chicks from hatching to 30 days. They showed no fear on the first day, and soon came to follow him. While the Sooty Terns approached at the sound of Watson's imitation 'peep', the Noddy Terns did not.

Wallace Craig (1908), following up Whitman's studies of behavioural and morphological traits of hybrid pigeons, noted, as had Whitman, that the young of one species reared under foster parents tended to mate with members of the foster species and later reported (1914) that male Ring-doves (*Streptopelia risoria*) reared in visual isolation, very often addressed masculine sexual displays to human beings. They gave up what Craig called the 'fetich' for human beings with difficulty, when associated with their own species.

Heinroth's important study of the Anatidae, published in 1911, reported many comparable findings which have since been followed up and extended by Lorenz (1935, 1937), who came to regard the acquisition of the imprint as marked by certain distinctive features. In summary, they were:

(i) The process is confined to a very definite and brief period in the life of the individual.

(ii) Once accomplished, the process is totally irreversible and in this respect is unlike ordinary, associative learning.

(iii) The imprinting process is often completed long before the behaviour, which suggests any patterning and rigidity, becomes discernible. Lorenz (1937) cites the case of a Musk Drake (*Cairina moschata*), hatched with four siblings by a pair of grey geese, which the drake followed for seven weeks. In all social activities, the bird associated with his own siblings; but when one year later his mating reactions began, they were addressed to the species of the foster parents which he had not seen for ten months.

(iv) The acquired imprint is generalised in the sense that the animal tends to react to the broad or general characteristics of the species upon which it may be imprinted.

Subsequent research, as will be shown, would suggest that (ii) might be modified; but it is relevant to note in passing that examples of analogous phenomena occur in several non-avian species.

Baerends (1950) followed up the earlier work of Noble and Curtis (1935, 1939), who had shown that male, cichlid fish which were reared in isolation for the early part of their life attempted to mate indiscriminately with members of either sex. Baerends worked mainly with the species *Hemichromis bimaculatus*, which spawn on the bottom, but made a number of observations on the closely related species *Tilapia natalensis*, which incubate the young in the mouth, and *Cichlasoma meeki*. He found that the young of *Hemichromis* (non-isolated) do not show the fright response during the first two days of free swimming. Using models which varied in type of movement, size, shape, texture, colour and pattern, it was found that stationary or rapidly moving models caused the fish to move away. Shape did not seem important; but size was, in that the young fish always followed at a distance which subtended the same angle with the object. Larger objects were followed at a greater distance. It is recalled that Lorenz when imprinting young goslings found that when he crouched, the birds approached till they observed the experimenter's head from the same angle. *Hemichromis* showed a marked preference for red; but in *Cichlasoma* the preference for red was not

apparent till after 15 days of age. With *Hemichromis*, a portion
of the sand at the bottom containing spawn was removed. The
female later returned to the correct spot and aerated for about
half an hour, before the response waned; but it could be
maintained if imitation eggs were inserted. Parents can recognise their own young, which they retrieve. When strange
young fish were introduced, however, they disappeared, apparently devoured. So too, inserted eggs of another species
quickly disappeared.

Bees also display a marked ability to acquire a very special-
ised response in a brief period in their early, mobile life. The
stark reality of survival dictates that in the short season when
nectar and pollen are available, no time be wasted. Studies by
von Frisch (1954) and Lindauer (1961) have shown that the
bees have evolved a method of maximising the return for
their effort. The worker bee who makes a rich find instructs
others as to its position by dancing either on the vertical face
of the comb or on a level space outside the entrance to the
hive. If the source of food is nearing exhaustion, no dance is
performed; but the individual forager will continue until
it is cleared. If the find is within 50–100 m from the hive, the
'round' dance is performed in which other workers may join.
The message is simply that a source of food corresponding to
the odour on the discoverer's body is available if the others,
who learn the message by joining in the dance, will search
around within a range of 50–100 m.

If the distance is beyond 100 m, the 'waggle' dance is performed. The bee executes a rough, figure-of-eight pattern and
the abdomen is waggled as the central portions are crossed.
As the distance of the food increases, the number of complete
waggle circuits per unit time decreases. Accurate timings of
the dance and the comparison of calculated distances, based
thereon, with measured distances between hive and food
source, have shown that accurate information as to distances
up to 11 km, or nearly 7 miles, can be gained by experienced
bees who join in the dance. If the dance is performed on a
vertical surface, a waggle run up the face means that the find
is in the direction of the sun. If the run is orientated, say, 10°

to the left of the vertical, that will be the operative bearing relative to the sun's position. Bees are confused in the dark, but can orientate quite successfully as long as some light (as little as 10° of blue sky through a chink in the hive) is available. Lindauer (1961) has shown that very few young bees forage until they have learned to follow a dance. Conditions are frequently crowded in or in front of the hive, and the young bees tend to follow the first dancer available and consequently to search at first for the type of pollen thus encountered. The tendency to follow is apparently innate, and the first attempts at following are very clumsy; but they improve, and so does the efficiency of the foraging.

Another phenomena analogous to imprinting has been suggested by Thorpe (1963) in respect of the Chaffinch (*Fringilla coelebs*). Birds hand-reared in isolation produce very simple songs corresponding to what are the inborn components of the song. If such birds are brought together, the ultimate song is highly abnormal. In the early weeks of their life, the young birds appear in normal circumstances to be able to acquire from their parents or other chaffinches singing nearby the basic features of the chaffinch song – for example, the division into phrases, the limits of pitch and that it should end with a flourish. Thorpe claims that there is good evidence that this auditory learning can occur both in the laboratory and in the wild, without immediate practice by the young bird. In the first breeding season, however, the bird sings in competition with other birds for territories and, in this way, learns the finer details and ornamentations of the song. As might be expected, chaffinches in different districts have slightly different songs and any ornithologist skilled in this field can detect the local style and accent without waiting for confirmation from the sound spectrograph. Fascinating though the work of Thorpe, Marler (1961) and others definitely is, it is tempting to quote an earlier worker: 'The kinds of sound capable of being produced are identical within the limits of one and the same species; but articulate sound, that one might reasonably designate "language", differs both in various animals, and also in the same species according to diversity of locality. . . . Of little birds, some sing a different note from the parent birds if they have been removed from the nest and heard other birds singing and a mother Nightingale has been observed to give lessons in singing to a young bird, from which spectacle we might obviously infer that the song of the bird was not equally congenital with mere voice, but was something capable of modification and refinement' (Aristotle, *Historia Animalium*, circa 340 B.C., Book IV, 9, 536b). In the case of the Chaffinch, hormonal changes have the result that beyond the age of 13 months, they are incapable of acquiring song patterns.

Among mammals, Klopfer *et al.* (1964) have demonstrated with goats and Smith *et al.* (1966) with sheep, that the mother acquires within a matter of minutes the olfactory impression which enables her to distinguish her own young. In a very sensitive study with children in Glasgow, Schaffer and Emerson (1964) have shown that there is a progression during an important critical period for the first six or eight months of infancy. At first the child reacts to social approaches by general activity. By two months the mother is recognised visually, by three months by her voice. Up to about six months the child will normally smile at most people, but thereafter less readily, except to those of close acquaintance.

But despite these similarities and the many more which could be pointed out, the terms *'einzuprägen'* and *'Die Prägung'* arose with Heinroth and Lorenz and have been largely associated with birds. It may have been that in dealing with ducks and geese, which in the author's experience imprint very quickly in comparison with, say, the domestic chicken, both Heinroth and Lorenz were impressed with the speed and irrevocability of the process, an impression which the image of 'imprinting' tends to perpetuate. But others were to take up the study. Nice (1953) and Fabricius (1951a, b) with ducklings and Hinde, Thorpe and Vince (1956) with Moorhens (*Gallinula chloropus*) and Coots (*Fulica atra*) obtained comparable results, further illustrating the basic validity of the earlier findings and serving as an introduction to the spate of experimentation which we are about to review.

3. The Initial Approach

At the outset, it may be stated that a great variety of intermittent stimuli will induce responses of approach in recently
hatched, precocial birds. If one takes a domestic chick (*Gallus
gallus*) about 20 hours after hatching, when the feathers are
quite dry and the tiny bird is capable of walking freely, it can
be attracted to the other side of the room by simply holding
one's hand in the path of the light and playing shadow patterns,
low down on the wall. As it approaches the intermittent
stimulus, the bird in most cases will give the low-pitched
contentment chirps and may peck on the ground near the
stimulus. Actually the pecking is an innate reaction and as yet
unrelated to the abatement of hunger, since the bird is provided naturally with reserves which will sustain it for the first
day or two. Alternatively, one could have attracted the chick
by dragging some object in front of it or by tapping lightly on
the floor. The essential feature is the embodiment of change.

Several workers have shown that the likelihood and extent
of the response of the young bird is greater if some change is
involved in nearby stimuli. Fabricius (1951b), working with
Tufted Ducks (*Aythya fuligula*), Eider Ducks (*Somateria
mollissima*) and Shoveler Ducks (*Spatula clypeata*), found that
the shape of his models did not seem to be very important.
Motion of the model appears necessary; but compared with a
smooth swimming motion, the movement was even more
effective if parts of the model moved, as would be the case
with the parent duck, relative to one another. The inclusion of
low-pitched and brief sounds with the model, such as the
words 'kom, kom', appreciably enhanced response, but sustained hissing sounds tended to evoke escape. Weidmann

(1958), working with Mallard Ducks (*Anas platyrhynchos*), reported very similar findings. His ducklings would not approach a motionless human being, but did so if the experimenter moved away slowly and swayed from side to side. The emission of short, low-pitched notes from an unseen source was conducive to movement; but long, sustained notes were ineffective. Weidmann noted among other things that ducklings isolated for 40 hours would not follow the model, but ducklings isolated for up to 50 hours would join other ducklings, or if they had not seen other ducklings, they would join newly hatched Moorhens or Pheasants. The implication is that up to a certain time the young bird will approach or follow a wide range of moving objects, but that some further experience of the object is necessary before attachment to a particular object or stimulus, with the implied ability to discriminate, can develop. This is in agreement with Fabricius' view, that young Tufted Ducks, Eiders, Shovelers and Mallards are not born with an innate image or 'schema' of the parent bird. The stimuli which can activate the innate releasing mechanism for approach and following are simple; but during the first reaction, the mechanism begins to become more selective by a process akin to conditioning. But the importance of motion in the stimulus object or stimulus situation does seem to be basic. Dimond (1965) used a model of a crow in one of his experiments. If it was kept in movement at one end of his test run, the chicks spent most of the time at that end of the run. It did not matter that the crow was upside down or otherwise, as long as it moved.

James (1959) and Smith (1960) were able to show with domestic chicks that very simple stimuli indeed could induce approach and attachment. Both found that a flickering patch of light would elicit the usual sequence of approach, contentment chirps, pecking in front of the stimulus and attachment. James (1959) and Abercrombie and James (1961) went on to show that intermittent light, flashing through small holes in the side of the run beside an object, could serve as the unconditioned stimulus to condition the chick to approach and become attached to the object. Tests up to the age of 12 days did not indicate any decline in the approach to the intermittent light. Smith (1962) also found that approach to a 12-inch-dia. circle of light projected intermittently on to a screen from the rear would elicit approaches up to the age of 90 days, although the response was waning after the twentieth day. A much more effective stimulus, both in eliciting initial approach and sustaining it, was found to be a 12-inch-dia. white disc with a 45° black sector painted thereon, rotating slowly at 1·5 revs per second (Smith, 1960) – see Plate IV. This again was significantly more attractive to the (Brown Leghorn × Light Sussex) chicks than the same disc, plus sector, moving directly away from the chick and not rotating. Expressed in another way, movement in the frontal parallel plane, i.e. at right angles to the chick's direct line of vision, was significantly more attractive than movement in the sagittal plane, i.e. straight ahead, or in direct line of regard, as one would fire an arrow. In separate tests, horizontal and vertical movement in the frontal parallel plane were found to be equally effective. A possibility suggested by the work of Maturana et al. (1960) and Maturana and Frenk (1963) is that separate cells of the bird's retina, which respond to movement in specific directions and mediate the detection of edges, are involved. A black sector on a white background, rotating in the frontal parallel plane, could conceivably activate many types of cells, thereby increasing the probability of response.

The explanation of why movement should be attractive to a young bird has been the topic of further speculation. Birds do not have the matrix of blood vessels which cover and serve to nourish the inner layers of the mammalian retina. Instead, they have a roughly conical pecten with folded layers on its surface which covers the 'blind-spot', i.e. the point where the optic nerve enters the retina. The apex of this cone points forward, towards the pupil of the eye. Menner (1938) demonstrated that the folds of the pecten throw shadows on the retina, thereby tending, by the fluctuation of shadows produced by a moving object, to maximise the animal's attention to that object. Quite possibly an object moving across the bird's line of vision would cast more shadows than one moving directly away in the saegittal plane. This would be an interesting experiment. Menner did show that the extent of the folding of the pecten and, in consequence, the variegation of the shadows, differed between species and was correlated with their mode of life. The most extensive range of shadows was produced on the retinas of hawks. Birds feeding by day on insects came next, and nocturnal birds had the simplest pattern of all. Menner concluded that the pecten was in some way related to the detection of movement and carried out a further experiment. He directed a camera at the clear sky where, high above him, some swifts were circling. On the ground glass focusing screen he could detect nothing. A model of the hawk's pecten was then stuck on the inside of the screen and he found that he could discern an image of the swifts. Menner's experiments would indicate that many birds who gather their food in the daylight are well equipped to detect and respond to movement. His results in themselves do not explain why at an early age, in the so-called 'critical period', moving objects elicit approach and following, which is more difficult or impossible to achieve when the bird is older.

Matthews and Hemmings (1963) have suggested that following, i.e. remaining near to a moving object, tends to increase the sensory input to the bird, and it might be supposed that an increase or the maintenance of a high level of sensory input could be more significant when the bird is very young and has little accumulated experience. A further theory has been suggested by Moltz (1960) to explain the development of sustained approach and following. He points to the observation by many workers that in the first few days of the bird's life there is little evidence of fear. Intermittent stimulation, mediated by the pecten, ensures that moving objects are 'attention getting' and for this reason the bird approaches. The stimulus object thus becomes associated with a state of low anxiety, so that when in later days fear does develop, the bird tends to follow the object associated with low anxiety.

Reasoning on these lines, Moltz (1963) describes the early following of an object as a 'selective learning process involving fear reduction', but inclines to the view that in the early stages the nature of the stimulus is perhaps more important. He cites data, for example, indicating that of groups of restrained chicks which were exposed to an approaching object, a retreating object, a stationary object and one alternatively approaching and retreating, those exposed to the retreating objects were significantly the best followers in tests 24 hours later, with no significant differences between the 'alternating' and 'approach' groups, and the 'stationary object' group, a bad last.

It is important, however, to note that attachment to an object can arise by a process of familiarisation. Hess (1959b) and Abercrombie and James (1961) have all drawn attention to this possibility, and Thorpe (1963) has pointed to the usefulness of a process of this kind in assisting the bird to know and orientate within its environment. Gray (1960) designed an experiment in which groups of White Rock chicks, maintained in visual isolation from other chicks, were exposed to motionless black, geometric shapes. Half the group were exposed to a circle $3\frac{1}{2}$ inches in dia. and the others to an equilateral triangle of side 4 inches. The objects were $\frac{3}{4}$ inch thick. Three separate groups of chicks were exposed for 24 hours to the objects, one group on the third day, the others on the fourth and fifth days of age, respectively. In final preference tests, using the criterion of time spent near the familiar model minus time near the unfamiliar model, the results in Gray's view were unequivocal. All groups revealed a significant preference for the familiar object. The preferences were calculated on the assumption that the two objects were of equal intrinsic attractiveness to the chicks and this could be debated and tested; but as Gray concedes, the objects did stand out from the background and any condition which ensures that a stimulus object captures attention, could mediate an attachment. Taylor and Taylor (1964) performed a similar experiment. When emerging dry from the incubator, half of their 32 chicks were transferred to individual boxes with a small cardboard box attached to the wall and the other half to identical boxes with an object made of foam rubber, suspended from a corresponding position. At the age of 48 hours, each object was placed at the opposite end of a small pen and the chick introduced at the centre. While 13 chicks gave none or unclassifiable responses, and one approached both, the remainder went exclusively to the familiar object, which was interpreted as a significant result. It was noted that the foam rubber received more pecks and that the chicks were more inclined to make contact with it, raising the interesting issue of whether or not tactile imprinting is possible in chicks (see Taylor *et al.*, 1967).

This 'passive' method of acquiring a preference and a measure of attachment suggests many further issues. Bateson (1964a) has shown that by rearing chicks in individual pens, with either black and white vertical stripes or yellow and red horizontal stripes, a significant difference in following for models bearing the familiar striping could be obtained; but there is the further problem of whether or not active association with the imprinting object would be more effective in the short and the long term, both in promoting following and discrimination.

COLOUR AND INTENSITY

Pumphrey (1948), reviewing the evidence, inclines to the view that there are no great differences in the colour vision of man and birds, although it is emphasised that because of the greater density of cones (cells mediating colour vision) relative to rods (which mediate black and white vision) on the periphery of the retina of the bird, colour should play a much more important role in the vision of birds which are active in daylight. Bateson (1964c) has shown, too, that static objects which appear most conspicuous to human vision are in fact approached more frequently by day-old chicks; but unfortunately, from a methodological point of view, many studies of colour in association with imprinting include the further variables associated with movement. Different methods of assessing the hue and reflectance of the coloured surfaces have also been used.

Schaefer and Hess (1959) working with Vantress Broiler chicks of White Rock stock and moving 7-inch-dia. spheres in different colours, reported an order of preference, from highest to lowest, of blue, red, green, orange, grey, black, yellow, white. Jaynes (1958) imprinted New Hampshire Red chicks upon a red object and tested their power to respond to pink, yellow, white and green objects. Over four days, the chicks developed an increasing responsiveness to the original red. The shape of the objects may have intruded; but the possibility of changes in responsiveness to different colours, with increasing age, does emerge. This possibility was demonstrated by Gray (1961) working with White Rock chicks. The stimuli were rotating solid circles, $5\frac{1}{2}$ inches dia., in colours black, white, red, green, blue and yellow rated to the nearest Otswald chips (a system of colour rating), grey scale p, grey scale a, 7·5 p.a., 22 p.i., 13·5 p.e. and 3 p.a., respectively, a further disc painted red on the upper two-thirds and yellow below, and a yellow chick of the same species. These were exposed to the chicks on each of the first five days of age. The chick was the only object evoking a significant response on the first day of life, possibly because of movement. Responses to red were significant on day 2 and day 3 but not on day 5. Yellow, black and red-yellow gave significant results on day 2. Thereafter there was a decline in response.

Smith and Hoyes (1961), working with (Brown Leghorn × Light Sussex) chicks aged 24 ± 6 hours, placed the stimuli 6ft from the chicks. In one experiment the stimuli were 6-inch-dia. circles of light, flashed on/off for $\frac{1}{2}$ second, behind a translucent screen via Wratten filters Red (29), Green (61) and plain white, all at an intensity of 0·43 foot-candles. At this age, there were no significant differences in the number of chicks approaching the stimulus. In another experiment, balls, swinging pendulum fashion through a constant arc, were painted red (Munsell rating 5·0R, 5–12), green (2·5G, 6–6) and plain white. Again, although the results did not attain significance, there were always slightly more responses to red. Smith and Bird (1964a), using the same strain of chicks and much the same technique, exposed 6-inch-dia. circles of light at a brightness of one lambert via Wratten filters Red (29), Green (61), Blue (47B), Yellow (9) and direct light from a domestic bulb. One trial was held on the first day of the chick's life and three trials for the next four days. Performance was assessed in the distance covered by the chick in the direction of the stimulus within a given time. Again there were no statistically significant differences on day 1, although red was on top. By day 5, however, there were significant differences. Red was significantly more effective than blue and white and so, too, were green and yellow (see Fig. 2).

Another experiment was performed with pendulum balls painted with colours on the Munsell scale, red (5·0R, 6–6), yellow (5·0Y, 6–6), yellow (5·0Y, 8–12), green (5·0G, 6–6), blue (5·0B, 6–6) – again over five days. There were no statistically

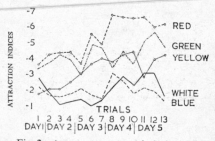

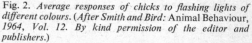

Fig. 2. *Average responses of chicks to flashing lights of different colours.* (*After Smith and Bird:* Animal Behaviour, *1964, Vol. 12. By kind permission of the editor and publishers.*)

significant differences between approaches to different colours, but red was again the most effective. However, when the 60 chicks involved were presented with a ball of an unfamiliar colour on the last day, there was a huge and statistically significant decline in the responses, indicating that some imprinting to colour had taken place.

Despite the many differences in experimental design, the consistent result emerging from the foregoing experiments, even when statistical significance is not attained, is the relatively great effectiveness of red. It is of interest to note Gray's (1961) observation that the female of the ancestral form of domestic chicks (*Gallus bankiva*) has a red breast.

In a further experiment to study the effect of intensity, Smith and Hoyes (1961) exposed chicks once only to one of two 6-inch-dia. discs of light, flashed intermittently through a projector on to the rear of a translucent screen. One disc was 'bright', giving a reading of 0·36 foot-candles, and the other 'dull' (0·002 foot-candles). The difference in brightness was obvious to human vision. The 'bright' disc attracted more full approaches, so many more in fact that the difference would only have occurred by chance 5 times in 10 000. In another experiment a comparison was made by focusing the light from the projector to a diameter of 2 inches for one series of exposures and to 6-inch-dia. for another. Differences in approach from a distance were not significant, suggesting that the small differences in visual angle were not crucial for initial approach when the total amount of light was approximately the same.

THE CONFORMATION OF THE STIMULUS

As might be expected in the early experimental approach to a phenomenon, there has been no great attempt to ensure that stimuli used to evoke approach and following are standardised. However, a tentative picture emerges. In a sensitive early study with Mallard ducklings at the reservation of the Wildfowl Trust at Slimbridge on the Severn estuary, Fabricius and Boyd (1953) obtained following responses to objects as small as a match-box. Hinde, Thorpe and Vince (1956) with Moorhens and Coots obtained following responses to objects varying widely in shape and ranging in size up to a large canvas 'hide'. With these birds, man in motion was found to be the most effective stimulus, possibly for the reason suggested by Smith's (1960) experiments, that motion in the frontal parallel plane, as would occur in the oblique view of the legs, is a very effective stimulus. It will be recalled that Fabricius (1951b) found movements of parts of the model, relative to one another, to be very effective. Hinde and his co-workers found that once the birds were following one object, they would readily generalise their response to another object. The range of stimuli which different species could generalise could be the topic of painstaking research. The evidence suggests that the range for some species might be wide; but the relationship of some important variables in perception and learning might be made clearer.

One important factor does appear to be the angle of regard between the bird and stimulus object. Moltz, Rosenblum and Stettner (1960) found that of 30 ducklings exposed to a stationary box (5 in × 3 in) at 7 inches distance, none subsequently followed; but of 24 exposed at 14 inches, 18 followed. Lorenz (1935), too, has indicated that to ensure following he has often had to stoop or adjust the distance between himself and the birds. Smith and Hoyes (1961) were also able to demonstrate the importance of visual angle in two simple experiments. In a circular run, objects were suspended from a radius arm to be different heights above the floor. Objects moving 'on the deck', i.e. not above 6 inches from the floor, were much more effective than those at greater heights. In another experiment, chicks approached from a distance a 3-inch-dia. flashing circle of light on a screen. One disc was 'on the deck', i.e. with centre 2 inches above the floor, and in a separate trial the disc was in the 'high' position, 20 inches above the floor. The low position was significantly more effective. The difference in angle of regard for the chick at the starting-point was 21°. It was noted that when approaching the 'high' position many chicks advanced, continually raising their heads until at about half distance, where they stopped and, with beaks raised upward as far as seemed possible, emitted loud 'fear' chirps.

AUDITORY STIMULI

Several workers, including Lorenz (1935), Fabricius (1951), Nice (1953), Collias and Collias (1956), Hinde, Thorpe and Vince (1956) and Weidmann (1958), have noted the considerable facilitating effect of auditory stimuli on the initial approach response of young birds. There is evidence that sound is not only attractive in itself, but may have a general facilitating effect on other responses. Tolman (1967), for example, has shown that an increase in the rate of feeding in three- to four-day-old cockerels can be obtained by tapping in the vicinity and that the increase tends to be correlated with the rate of tapping. Pitz and Ross (1961), working with Vantress Broiler chicks from the age of 12 to 15 hours post-hatch, in trials extending over five days, found that the sounding of a clapper on the first three days resulted in a significantly better following performance as compared with controls. They concluded that while the performance of the chicks varied widely, the general enhancement was due to greater arousal.

Klopfer (1959a, b) found that the surface nesting species, Mallards and Redheads (*Aythya americana*), if reared in auditory isolation, tended to approach most rhythmic sounds without discrimination. Wood Ducks (*Aix sponsa*), a hole-nesting species, however, rapidly developed a tendency to approach a repeated pattern of sound and that pattern alone, i.e. to imprint auditorily. Muscovy Ducks (*Cairina moschata*), on the other hand, showed virtually no tendency to respond to sounds. In a series of experiments, Klopfer tested the possibility that another hole-nesting species, the Sheld-duck (*Tadorna tadorna*), would show some auditory imprinting. He found little evidence of this, but that the birds could develop a preference for a sound if it was associated with a visual model which they had followed for a time and thus 'learned' in context. Gottlieb (1963a) inclines to the view that in a ground-nesting species the chief function of the mother's calls is one of arousal or 'attention getting'; but in a hole-nesting species such as the Wood Duck, the auditory stimuli have a different role. They are, in the darkness and restriction of the nest-hole, the chief and possibly the only method of recognising the mother. The Wood Duck mother begins to vocalise as soon as the eggs are 'pipped'. The intensity of these low 'kuk-kuk' calls increases and so does the noise from the newly hatched ducklings, as the time for the exodus from the nest approaches. If no potential predators are about, the duck drops to the water below and begins calling. One after another, the ducklings climb up to the rim of the entrance hole and tumble out and down to the water, a distance which may vary up to 60 ft. When no more calls issue from the nest above, the duck swims off with the brood. Clearly, in such circumstances, it is of greater survival value for the young to be auditorily imprinted on the mother's calls than on other sounds, or to be visually imprinted on a mother whom they cannot see on the water below them. See Plates IIa and IIb.

Another interesting observation on the same problem is offered by Klopfer and Gottlieb (1962a) in respect of the wild Mallard ducklings, which are incubated in nests on the ground and follow the hen through the reeds and bushes to the water. They incubated 100 eggs of wild Mallards, sent to them from the Delta Waterfowl Research Station in Manitoba, and maintained the ducklings in darkness before the experiment so that they had auditory and tactile, but no visual, experience. In training sessions of 20 minutes beginning at the age of 6 to 24 hours, the birds followed in a circular run a model of a male Mallard equipped with a speaker on the underside, emitting the sounds 'kom, kom'. In phase I of the crucial tests, the ducklings were presented with a silent moving model, which in phase II was removed from the run, while the 'kom kom' call issued from two side alleys in the run. They found no consistent relationship between the age of the birds and the predominance of either the visual or the auditory modality; but they did find that some birds responded better to the auditory and others had a preference for the visual stimuli. This was termed 'behavioural polymorphism' and its applications are of interest. They suggest that those birds which hatch first in a batch may be the ones with the auditory preference. Reasons why this may be so will be discussed in the next chapter; but for a species which has to pass through undergrowth with only intermittent visual experience of the mother, the polymorphism is claimed to have some advantages. The authors claim that the leadership in a group of these ducklings is changing constantly and is independent of any relationship of dominance. If some members of the group respond best to sound, and these might be those who hatched early and became well imprinted on the mother's calls before the exodus from the nest, and others respond best to visual stimuli, then there is an enhanced probability that the cohesion of the group as a whole will be maintained. A behavioural polymorphism of this sort, they write, 'enables the group as a whole to perform at the level of its best performers.'

In another similar experiment, Klopfer and Gottlieb (1962b) found again that, while a minority of their Mallard ducklings scored highly both in response to visual and auditory stimuli, the majority only obtained high scores as auditory responders, while a small number registered their best performance with visual stimuli. In this experiment, Gottlieb's (1961a, 1963b) technique of dating the age of the chick from the onset of incubation was used, giving the peak period of following between 27 days 12 hours and 27 days 23 hours of developmental age. Gottlieb feels that this is a more reliable indication of the true state of development of the bird because 'important neurophysiological and neuromuscular developments relevant to imprinting take place somewhat independently of hatching.'

It is of interest to note that Smith and Bird (1964c) found with another species, (Brown Leghorn × Light Sussex) chickens, that over the second to the fourth day of life, post-hatch, the correlation between auditory and visual responsiveness is low but positive and statistically significant, in the sense that it is greater than could be attributed to chance. They also found that the subsequent response to visual stimuli was better for those chicks which encountered an auditory stimulus first, an observation which accords with the suggestion that the auditory stimulation has a general function of arousal. One impressive function of auditory stimuli was, however, clearly apparent in another experiment by Smith and Bird (1964c) with small flocks of chicks. In such groups, each chick presents a very attractive stimulus combination to the other chicks. It embodies movement in all planes, different colours and light reflected from feathers and eyes. In consequence, the young birds take only desultory notice of an experimental visual stimulus with which it is hoped to attract them. In the moment that intermittent sound is associated with the visual stimulus, however, the behaviour of the group changes and they tend to move in the direction of the stimulus combination. A previously trained 'leader', i.e. a chick already imprinted, will also improve the approach of a tardy group.

Collias and Joos (1953) have by the use of the sound spectrograph, made a very thorough analysis of the sounds which attract the domestic chick. The attractive sounds are of low pitch, i.e. below a frequency of 800 cycles per second, with optimum response occurring between 49 and 392 c/s. A pattern must be well segmented, with brief component notes, and is more effective if frequently repeated. Warning signals made by fowls are opposite in character. They are sustained, higher in pitch and reveal less repetition. Schwartzkopf (1955) has suggested that the chicks' differential reaction to low-pitched sounds is due to a developmental stage in the middle ear. The adult hen after all responds to the high-pitched 'fear' chirps (above 3000 c/s) of the chick; but, whatever the reason, several empirical studies have shown that the properties indicated by Collias and Joos are effective over a wide range of species. Gottlieb (1963d) working with Mallards and beginning at a development age of 27 days, used a multi-coloured decoy with Mallard conformation emitting from an enclosed speaker the exodus call of the Wood Duck. Those exposed to the same decoy when it was silent, responded significantly worse. Smith and Bird (1963b) working with (Brown Leghorn × Light Sussex) chicks in tests from day 1 to day 6 in age, found that while visual and low-pitched auditory stimuli were both effective alone, the combination of the two produced a significantly better result, which by the second day had attained almost 100% response and was maintained.

The results obtained by Fischer (1966) also stressed the overall importance of auditory stimuli. She worked with commercial (White Giant × Pitch Broiler) chicks beginning at the approximate age, post-hatch, of 24 hours. The model was an 8-inch red cube emitting the recorded, brooding cackles of a bantam hen and some tapping. All the chicks were trained or imprinted on this model. The first 102 chicks to follow successfully were then tested with a variety of combinations, in which the familiar sounds were presented alone or in combination with the familiar object or with strange objects. The results showed quite clearly that whatever the visual component, it was only when the 'parent sound' was involved that performance equalled that attained in training sessions.

Reflection, in the light of the foregoing experimental findings, will indicate that the hen in natural circumstances is very nearly, if not the maximally effective perceptual combination for inducing approach. She embodies, with her swaying gait and pecking movements, motion in the sagittal and frontal parallel planes, contrary motions within the surface of her body with associated changes in colour patterns, together with simultaneous sounds of maximum attractiveness. From a psychological point of view she embodies a high degree of perceptual redundancy, since any one of these features would be sufficient to initiate approach and following. When the young do follow, there are the further rewards or reinforcements of increased likelihood of food, warmth and protection. Furthermore, if they don't follow, mother has been observed to go back and nudge them along. It is but one example of an oft-repeated observation, that wherever in nature there is an issue of survival, evolutionary development has made more than adequate or at least more than the minimum provision.

FACTORS PREDISPOSING RESPONSE TO PARTICULAR TYPES OF STIMULI

Simner (1966) has produced experimental evidence that flickering light, presented to the chick at rates corresponding to the foetal heart-beat, provoke better approach responses than other rates, when the chicks are tested at 8, 26, 50 and 76 hours after hatching. He has also shown that the likelihood of vocal activity in the newly hatched chick is greater when the chick's heart rate decreases towards the rate which had operated in embryo. Further evidence of association between foetal activity and later behaviour has been provided by Gottlieb (1965a). In natural circumstances, the head of the chick and duck embryo moves into the air space at the large end of the egg some days before hatching. The embryo then begins to utter peeps of low intensity. The incubating duck is also known to utter calls of very low intensity during this period before hatching. By inserting fine electrodes into the lower part of the bill of the embryo on the day before hatching, Gottlieb was able to obtain objective records of bill or beak clapping before hatching. The behaviour of the foetus was then studied when maternal calls of their species were played on a tape, for periods of 30 seconds, at an intensity about 70 decibels. Vocalisation by the foetus was recorded on a very sensitive microphone. Results were very significant. The embryos always responded by beak clapping and vocalisation between the bursts of recorded sound. In later experiments, Gottlieb (1966) showed that White Rock chicks and Peking ducklings which were visually isolated after hatching but could hear their own noises and those of other recently hatched birds, followed models emitting adult calls of their species in preference to other models emitting juvenile calls. The same was true in the great majority of cases of naïve, artificially incubated ducklings which, because of auditory isolation had no experience of maternal or sibling calls. In another group, exposure to recordings of juvenile calls actually increased the response to adult calls of their own species, but not to those of another species, namely the exodus call of the Wood Duck. Reviewing the general development of behaviour in the duck embryo, Gottlieb and Kuo (1965) stress the continuity bet-ween activity of the embryo and later behaviour, and Gottlieb (1967) has provided further specific illustration. Up to three days before hatching (normally after 27 days of incubation in Mallards), the embryo responds to recordings of maternal calls of its own species by oral activity, i.e. by behavioural activity. On the other hand, it responds physiologically (in-crease in heart rate) to the calls of all duck species. To illus-trate further, Gottlieb isolated eggs from all sound at day 23 of incubation and tested the embryo's response at day 26 to the maternal call of the species. They did *not* respond be-haviourally (bill clapping or vocalisation) but they did show physiological activation – see Plate I.

The evidence available from Gottlieb's experiments to-gether with that from studies by Peters *et al.* (1958, 1963) and

Paulsen (1965) would appear to indicate that while auditory, visual, muscular and circulatory systems of the chick and duck embryo are capable of activation before hatching, the auditory system becomes responsive to specific stimulation earlier than the visual system. A result which is difficult to interpret, nevertheless, is that of Dimond (1966) who found that chicks incubated in darkness were much more likely to follow a moving red balloon at the age of 36 hours, post-hatch, than those incubated in light, who in fact showed more aversion to the object.

Of considerable interest in this context are the observations of Vince (1964, 1966a, b) who has recorded two rhythms from eggs of several species of quail, a hatching rhythm which consists of sounds of relatively large amplitude, and 'clicking' which sets in some 20 to 12 hours before hatching, i.e. between the pipping of the egg and hatching. Eggs of the different species of quail have a characteristic number of clicks per minute, e.g. the Bob-white Quail (*Colinus virginianus*), 82–160, and the Japanese Quail (*Coturnix coturnix japonica*), 61–196. By putting eggs 'late' into a clutch of other incubating eggs, Vince found that while the time of pipping was unaffected, the time between their pipping and hatching could be shortened, presumably because of the stimulation deriving from the clicking of nearby eggs. With the highly mobile broods of quail, survival would be favoured if the whole clutch of eggs hatched within a short period and the brood was then able to move off as a whole and, in the total pattern of stimulation, the noises made by the mother should not be ruled out. In a later study, in which artificial stimulation of the incubating eggs was included, it was found that in most cases the stimulated egg hatched first and clutches of eggs in contact did in fact hatch within six hours; but isolated eggs hatched over a much longer period – 46 hours in the case of the Bob-whites, and 63 hours for the Japanese Quail. While the mechanism and circumstances are different, it has been noted by Carr and Hirth (1961), in tests made at Costa Rica, that social facilitation is vital to the hatching and emergence of the young of the Green Turtle (*Chelonia mydas*) from the nest in the sand

and in reaching the sea. Single young have a very poor chance even of emerging from the sand; but with larger numbers of eggs, from 50 to 100, the percentage emerging often approached and even attained 100%.

SOCIAL FACTORS AND RESPONSIVENESS

A newly hatched chick or duckling, as shown above, has already been subject to some auditory and possibly diffuse visual stimulation before hatching. On becoming a member of a brood, it is exposed to many additional forms of stimulation, apart from those deriving from the mother, such as bodily contact and auditory and visual stimuli from other chicks. These conceivably could influence responsiveness both directly, by ensuring a higher general state of arousal, and indirectly, by the effect on the emotional state of the bird. Some of these possibilities have been submitted to experimental test. Thompson and Dubanoski (1964b) demonstrated that Vantress Broiler chicks handled in the dark at the age of five hours, post-hatch, were significantly better at following the familiar object, in subsequent tests, than their controls or those handled at nine hours. Collins (1965) exposed 26 White Rock and 64 Leghorn chicks, maintained in isolation, to three conditions for 60 minutes at the age of 48 hours, viz. following and contact with the model, following and no contact, and no following and no contact. The imprinting object was a moving, half-sized model of a hen. Crucial tests were held five days later and scored with reference to orientation towards the model and proportion of time spent within half the radius of the model. All three experimental groups were better than naïve controls; but the differences between the groups were very small. While the group permitted following and contact performed best, the group allowed no following and contact was second. Collins concluded that neither contact nor following was essential for imprinting; but apparently he did not conduct any discrimination tests to prove that the birds had achieved a definite attachment.

Further indications of the influence of social conditions have been provided by Guiton (1958), who found that Brown

Leghorn chicks which had been housed as a group showed a marked decline in the tendency to follow a strange moving object at the age of 72 hours. Isolated chicks, however, did not reveal the same decline, and communally reared birds which had ceased to follow could be induced to follow again if maintained in isolation for a few days. It was noted, too, that the addition of sound to the model would often induce following in an unresponsive bird. In a later experiment, Guiton (1959) found that while the initial following response of isolates was poorer, it soon surpassed that of socially housed birds. The response of isolates was, however, better if their isolation was interrupted by a few hours of social experience. Again, a period of isolation extending up to three days, if inserted after following had been established to a particular object, did appear to assist the process of generalisation, i.e. the transfer of the response to another moving object.

Guiton's findings are of particular interest because they indicate, as Sluckin and Salzen (1961) have affirmed, that in natural conditions the process of imprinting may be brought to a close by following becoming more exclusively attached to a particular stimulus object. Again, it is possible to speculate that the early, crude, undifferentiated response to follow almost any moving object is dissipated earlier in socially reared chicks by minor imprintings on one another and before the development of fear, which could ensure that any established attachment was later held even more definitely.

Whatever the explanation, there are several studies which indicate that isolated young birds in comparable circumstances respond more readily than socially reared birds. James (1960) using flashing light as the stimulus, reported significantly better approach scores from isolates which encountered the stimulus at about 48 hours of age, in trials extending over five days. Sluckin and Salzen (1961) reported results broadly consistent with those of Guiton. Isolates responded better in tests conducted on the first day and more markedly on the fifth day. Those reared socially for the first six hours of life and then isolated for the rest of the day followed significantly better than both the isolates and socially housed. Polt and Hess

(1964) found that different groups of Vantress Broiler chicks, isolated in darkness and then given two hours in fluorescent light with 10 chicks of their own age before exposure to models at the age of 16 and 36 hours, showed a greater improvement in response than those merely exposed to light for a similar period. They reported a high correlation between following, and discrimination of strange and familiar models, only for socially housed chicks and their controls at the age of 16 hours. In a later study with 370 Vantress chicks, they had two major groups. One group were isolates, of which different sub-groups at 16, 24, 36 and 48 hours, post-hatch, were exposed to a blue 8-inch-dia. ball equipped with a speaker. The other major group was exposed to the same model in sub-groups for each of the above ages but had a period of two hours in a brooder with 10 chicks of the same hatch just before being exposed to the model. Among the isolates, those encountering the model at the age of 16 hours were significantly the best; but they did not do as well as the social group at 16 hours of age, or indeed at any other age. It was noteworthy that at successively greater ages, the performance of the isolated groups declined, whereas that of the social groups tended to increase. Hess in another study (1964), however, found that Mallard ducklings performed rather worse for social experience, and Klopfer and Gottlieb (1962b) found the same with Peking ducklings, the domesticated form of the Mallard.

Another aspect of social conditions is what might be regarded as the amount of learning which takes place. Schein and Hale (1959) accelerated the sexual development of Turkey poults by injections of testosterone propionate and tested the reactions to models of a poult's head, a stuffed poult body, a human hand, a wooden block and other objects. Some isolated poults displayed to inanimate objects, but none of those housed in groups did so. Again, whereas the responses of the isolated birds were predominantly to the observer's hand, those of the poults living in groups were all to the model of a poult's head. W. Smith (1957) has also shown that for White Leghorn and Barred Rock cockerels, which have been housed together in a brooder for eight days, a chick of the same breed can serve as a lure and that a pair of chicks will approach faster than a single chick. Broom (1966) studying the changes in behaviour of isolated chicks and small groups of chicks to a novel experience, the switching on of a 6-volt torch bulb in their home pen, came to the conclusion that both showed similar patterns of behaviour but that the socially housed chicks tended to show them earlier.

Clearly, social conditions are an important factor associated with responsiveness; but further work is required to clarify the relationships for different species, various stimuli and degree of domestication.

THE EFFECTS OF TEMPERATURE

Kaufman and Hinde (1961) demonstrated with White Leghorn and Rhode Island Red chicks that distress calls occur at a higher rate if the chick is placed in a strange run where the temperature is below the body temperature of the bird. Chicks maintained socially at 110° F, which would be regarded as a very comfortable temperature, increase their distress calling and significantly so, after the third day, when separated from their companions. This suggests some association between age and the development of fear, since isolated chicks under the same conditions do not record a significant increase with age.

Salzen and Tomlin (1963) suggested the possibility that a cold chick may be in a state of fear which could affect the following response. They compared the performance of two small groups of chicks. One group had been taken direct from the incubator where the temperature would normally be 103° F. The other group had been left in the colder room so that the chicks were cold to touch when tested. In a second experiment, a group of chicks were left in the room at 65° F and compared in performance with those taken directly from the incubator. The temperature in the testing enclosure where the chicks encountered a moving object was 75° F. The chicks ranged in age from 12 to 24 hours. In general, the cold chicks were slower to follow, but after 10 to 15 minutes the differences tended to disappear. The authors concluded that the influence of cold was mainly upon general motor activity and less probably upon perceptual and emotional processes. Klopfer and Hailman (1964a) applied cold shocks ($40 \pm 5°$ F) to young Peking ducklings immediately after and 6 to 16 hours after exposure to plain and gaudy models. In later tests of discrimination, they found no significant differences from controls in respect of the temperature variable.

4. Attainment of Attachment and Discrimination

While a variety of stimuli will induce approach and following in young nidifugous birds, the distinctive feature of imprinting is the establishment of a preference whereby over a period of time, the bird follows or remains attached to one object or type of object and does not respond in the same way to perceptually different objects. Clearly, there are many points in the process where differences of degree rather than sharply defined categories must be considered. Many studies have indicated that birds already following one object can generalise and respond in the same way to objects differing fairly widely from the one originally approached. Again, if the imprint and thus the preference is not established instantaneously, at first sight, it must be acquired over time, however short, and thus arises the obvious question of how, if at all, imprinting differs from any other process of acquisition or learning. A large number of precocial young, such as lambs, kids, foals, calves, hinds and camel calves as well as many birds, will approach the nearest large object in the vicinity upon becoming mobile, and if this proves to be comforting or reassuring, or in any way 'reinforcing' – in the language of learning theorists – continued attachment could be envisaged.

E. H. Hess (1959b, 1964) has asserted that imprinting is not to be identified with associative learning. His reasons are briefly:

(i) Massed practice rather than spaced practice, which is usually more effective in associative learning, and the actual

39

amount of effort (not time) expended in acquiring the discrimination are important and distinctive of imprinting.
The latter was demonstrated by moving the imprinting
object appreciably further in a given time for an experimental group and the insertion at times of obstacles in
the bird's path. This distinctive feature was summarised in
the Law of Effort namely, strength of imprinting = logar-
ithm of effort expended by the animal during imprinting.

(ii) The administration of certain drugs, e.g. meprobamate
and carisprodol, to chicks and ducklings does not depress
their ability to acquire or learn a simple colour discrimination with the reinforcement or reward of food; but these
drugs do appear to inhibit the process of imprinting, though
not apparently the retention of imprinting already established. Animals imprinted normally but tested under the
influence of the drugs are claimed to exhibit the usual effects
of imprinting.

(iii) In associative learning, recency favours retention of
what is acquired; but in imprinting, the features encountered first, i.e. the factor of primacy is more important.

(iv) Pain or shock, which in most experiments in associative learning incline the animal to avoid the objects encountered in association with the pain, tend on the other
hand to strengthen imprinting.

(v) 'True' imprinting can only take place within the so-
called 'critical period', which is claimed to be from hatching
to 32 or 36 hours for chicks and ducklings. Approach and
attachment achieved beyond this period are, in a somewhat
ex cathedra manner, described as associative learning.

Clearly, Hess has implied that the discriminatory response
which is characteristic of imprinting is acquired and is a form,
albeit a peculiarly distinctive form, of learning. He has con-
ceded (1959b) that it is a special form of learning which enables
the bird to learn the rough generalised characteristics of the
object and that the appreciation of the specific details which
come later have more in common with associative learning.

In the experiments which Hess has conducted in support of

his hypothesis, it is difficult to avoid some confounding of the variables. For an animal which is required to expend greater effort to be near a moving object, the maintenance of proximity could be associated with a greater state of anxiety which might have some influence upon the significance of the experience and subsequent retention. Again, it is conceivable that the greater effort expended may involve a greater number of occasions when the bird sees and hears the object from a slightly different orientation, and thus comes to know it better or to experience the greater attraction of an object which, while basically the same, is varying constantly within narrow limits. Further, as Sluckin and Salzen (1961) have pointed out, increasing the speed of the imprinting object to require greater effort in effect presents the duckling with a different and, in the experience of Lorenz, a more attractive stimulus. To date, very few experimenters have carried out a careful psycho-metric scaling of stimuli to decide the intrinsic attraction of stimuli. The phrase 'strength of imprinting' is of doubtful value if the familiar or unfamiliar stimulus differ in intrinsic attraction. A bird might, for example, form a strong attach-ment to an attractive stimulus with comparatively little expenditure of time and effort. One general feature emerging from all of Smith's experiments (1960 *et seq.*) is a positive correlation between the readiness of early approaches and speed and accuracy of subsequent discrimination. Beyond a certain point, expenditure of further time and effort may not appreciably enhance discrimination.

Baer and Gray (1960), for example, have shown that a statistically significant discrimination could be achieved with almost the minimum of movement. They used four groups of eight White Rock chicks. On each of the first four days after hatching, members of one of these groups were placed indi-vidually in a 6 in × 6 in box with a glass panel. Through this panel, four members of the group, as individuals, could see a white Guinea Pig; the others saw a black one. The chicks spent 24 hours in the boxes, and were tested seven days later in a 30-minute test in an apparatus in which their preference for either colour of Guinea Pig could be recorded by a system of micro switches. The best performance was recorded by the two-day old chicks. The authors concede that the discrimination is a simple one and that a normal process of imprinting would embrace finer details. Again, it could be argued that the exposure period of 24 hours brings the process nearer to habituation than imprinting. A significant degree of discrimination was established without following; but results of other studies suggest that it might have been established more quickly with greater movement.

Jaynes (1958a), for example, found that groups of New Hampshire Red chicks which received training periods of 5, 10, 20 and 40 minutes in following a silent green cube over the first four days of life, performed in retention tests at 30 days and at 70 days in proportion to the time spent in practice. Moltz, Rosenblum and Stettner (1960) divided their Peking ducklings into two major groups, an 'alley' group which was free to move in the test run and a 'restrained' group which had a full view of the training alley through a glass panel but was restricted in movement. Both major groups were further subdivided into those exposed to a moving test object, a stationary test object and no object at all. Training trials of 25 minutes were conducted on each of the first three days of life, and there were crucial discrimination tests, between the familiar and a strange object, on days 4 and 5. Movement was found to be very important. All those exposed to a moving object performed significantly better than those exposed to a stationary object or the empty alley; but there were no significant differences between the free, moving 'alley' group and the 'restrained' group and thus no support for the hypothesis of effort.

Essentially similar results were obtained by Smith (1962) in two experiments with (Brown Leghorn × Light Sussex) chicks. In the first, the chicks were exposed individually to a 6-inch-dia. flashing circle of light at a distance of 3 ft 6 in, the experimental group being restrained in a carefully fitted and padded box, with only the head protruding in the direction of the stimulus. Controls were free to approach the stimulus repeatedly for the same length of time, 8 minutes per day for the first three days. In the second experiment, a more powerful stimulus, a black sector painted on a white 12-inch-dia. rotating disc, was used. The experimental group was placed in a small cubicle, the front wall of which was transparent plastic. The box was large enough for the chick to turn around freely and peck at the bare floor. The controls were free to approach from a distance of 6 ft for the same time, three trials of three minutes per day for the first five days. Neither experiment provided any significant differences in the crucial tests, either in respect of following or discrimination. One interesting observation was that the chicks confined behind the plastic window probably saw less of the stimulus than the free-running controls. They frequently turned their back on the stimulus and, like many young chicks, seemed more interested in pecking in the rear corners of the cubicle.

Klopfer and Hailman (1964a) were interested in the subsequent effects of exposure of Peking ducklings to plain and striking models of adult ducks in association with the administration of cold shocks. They concluded from their observations, however, that following the models helped in later discrimination, but that 'neither the subsequent choice nor amount of subsequent following are direct functions of the amount of initial following' and in consequence they favoured 'repeal of the Law of Effort'. A novel variation on the theme of effort was introduced by Rice (1962), who divided his 8- to 28-hour-old Vantress Broiler chicks into three groups. Those in group 1 were free to follow individually a blue ball, 7 inches dia., fitted with a peeping loud-speaker. Members of group 2 were attached to the ball by a flexible rubber collar and a 12-inch length of string and were dragged along behind the ball for 100 ft, the distance required of group 1. Group 3 was a control group and received no training at all. In a discrimination test on their fourth day of life, the chicks were confronted with the choice between a live hen and the blue ball. Group 1 were significantly the best, but group 2 made significantly more approaches to the training object than group 3, and significantly more than chance. Many of them snuggled against the training object in the discrimination tests and gave contentment chirps, although during training they resisted being pulled along and gave loud distress calls.

A specific attempt to test the Law of Effort was made by Thompson and Dubanoski (1964a), working with Vantress Broiler chicks which were commercially hatched and housed in individual cages. The imprinting object was a blue and yellow doll, and for surrogates a stuffed hen and a toy duck were used. In a circular run the model was moved through 6 revolutions at a speed convienient for individuals of one group of chicks with a maximum time of 30 minutes. Members of a second group of chicks were placed in a plastic box which rotated with the model of the stuffed hen. Individuals of a third group were exposed for six minutes to the stationary model at a distance of 1 ft. In a second experiment, another surrogate, a blue and yellow toy duck, was followed by individuals of one group for 10 minutes and the distance noted. Members of a second group were placed in a plastic box and rotated with the model for a matched distance in the same time. Individuals of a third group were exposed to the stationary surrogate for 10 minutes. Crucial tests were held at 24 and 48 hours in the first experiment, and at 38 and 62 hours of age in the second. Locomotion by the chick's own effort gave significantly the best results in both following and discrimination. Responses by those exposed to the stationary object were weakest of all. In a third experiment, the conditions of locomotion by the chick – chick stationary/surrogate moving, and surrogate stationary/chick stationary – were compared. Locomotion by the chick again gave significantly the best results in following. Apparently no discrimination tests were held. The authors concluded that although the results were in favour of the hypothesis of effort, it does not necessarily follow that effort in itself is the chief cause of the enhanced performance. Following could be provocative of greater general arousal, attention to the imprinting object and reinforcement.

All of these possibilities could be further investigated along with variations of the perceptual characteristics of the imprinting object. As a point of interest, Lewis (1964) found that of two groups of female albino rats, those which had dragged heavy weights over a pulley to get at food tended by the third day to run faster than those which pulled light weights, and they also ate more even when nearly satiated.

On the evidence available, the hypothesis of effort raises several intriguing and unsolved problems of perception and learning. But, as yet, it is essentially an hypothesis and will remain of debatable standing until, with the aid of psychometric scaling, valid preference tests are constructed in each of the relevant sensory modalities.

THE INFLUENCE OF DRUGS

The evidence of the effect of drugs on imprinting is not particularly clear, probably because many drugs have side effects to their main function. Hess (1957) claimed that he was able to ensure imprinting in Mallard ducklings at an age when, because of the development of fear, their responsiveness is declining. A low anxiety state was held to be induced by the administration of chlorpromazine and meprobamate to ducklings between the age of 24 and 32 hours which were exposed to the imprinting object. When the effects of the drug had worn off, the birds were found to be more responsive than control animals to which water or nembutal had been administered. Hess (1959b) showed that meprobamate (25 mg/kg) and nembutal (5 mg/kg) appear to depress performance when the birds are presumed to be operative, but those imprinted normally at age 16 hours and later tested under the influence of the drugs performed quite well. Chlorpromazine (15 mg/kg) did not drastically lower performance at any phase. Elsewhere, Hess (1964) has argued that the drugs carisprodol and meprobamate, which are claimed to function as muscle relaxants, depress following responses and, by reducing effort, diminish the amount of imprinting. It is difficult to imagine that the eye musculature and general vigilance would not be affected, and more rigorous quantitative tests at all stages would be helpful.

Much clearer are the results reported by Kovach (1964) with different groups of Vantress Broiler chicks at the ages of 8, 14,

18, 24 and 32 hours, post-hatch. The stimulus was a blue ball 6·5 inches dia. with an internal speaker emitting the phrase 'come chick'. Administration of the drugs amphetamine or ephedrine was associated with a better response than controls up to the age of 18 hours, but not thereafter. Epinephrine was associated with poorer results at all ages, and so were neostigmine and atropine. Hexamethonium and ergonovine gave better results at nearly all ages, and though the performance appeared to be falling at 32 hours it was still above that of the controls. James (1962), using flickering light as the stimulus, found that injections of 5 mg of testoterone cyclopentylpropionate on the day of hatching or with chicks already imprinted to the flicker for five days had no effect. The same dosage administered to the chick when three days old, however, depressed the response to flicker.

Moving in another direction, Gutekunst and Youniss (1963) exposed their New Hampshire Red chicks, in two 5-minute sessions at the age of 24 hours, to a 2-inch green cube, which they followed. Three groups of chicks were then anaesthetised, one group immediately after the training session and the others at 15 minutes and 30 minutes thereafter, respectively. On recovery, the birds were returned to their home boxes; 24 hours later, similar trials were held. The results fell slightly short of statistical significance, but the overall picture was that the sooner the anaesthesia was applied the greater was the loss in responsiveness.

Once again it may be claimed that the action of drugs on imprinting will be better understood when, by psychometric scaling of stimuli in the relevant modalities, the specific effects of particular drugs can be accurately assessed. Since perceptual, emotional and motor factors appear to be involved, the action of particular drugs will require much detailed work.

SHOCK AND EXTERNAL REWARD

In many learning experiments with rats, a patterning of the animals' responses can be secured by rewarding one response and applying some kind of painful stimulation, such as a mild electric shock, when another response occurs. James and

Binks (1963) gave New Hampshire Red chicks of different ages mild electric shocks if they were standing in a white section of a testing box when the light came on. They found that no chicks at one day of age and only one at two days 'learned' to take avoiding action. By day 3, however, a larger number were avoiding the shocks, and the majority by day 5.

A broadly similar story emerges from the study of Fischer and Campbell (1964) with male Leghorn chicks. At one end of a narrow 4 ft runway, a group of chicks of the same age as the subject bird were visible in a cage. The subject was placed at the other end of the run. In the centre was a grid wired to a power source. Separate groups of 12 chicks were tested on day 3 to day 7, post-hatch. Acquisition trials consisted of exposing and, when necessary, prodding unresponsive chicks along and continued until they approached and jumped into the cage within one minute. Thirty seconds after the last acquisition trial, the subject was again placed at the former starting point with wet feet and the power switched on. Trials went on until the bird had either not crossed the grid in 5 minutes or had crossed it 15 times. The acquisition of both the social approach and the avoidance response improved markedly for chicks tested between day 3 and day 6, the most significant rise appearing at day 4. Schaller and Emlen (1962) carried out tests of avoidance to a 5 in × 9 in black rectangle with visually restricted isolates, isolates with visual experience of people, visually restricted pairs and visually experienced pairs, using a large number of domestic and wild species including ducks, turkeys, geese, pheasants and quail, and found, consistently with the other experimenters, that avoidance begins to increase after the first 10 hours of life. Strangeness of the object was thought to be the most important feature promoting avoidance. Thus, if an object is encountered before avoidance has developed, it will not subsequently induce marked avoidance.

Kovach and Hess (1963) fitted their experimental Vantress Broiler chicks with small electrodes under the wings and studied the influence of electric shocks (3 milli-amps for 5 seconds) upon the following of a blue ball, emitting the recorded 'come chick' phrase. When not in the experimental run, all the birds were housed in visual isolation. The birds of the experimental groups received 11 shocks during the process of following the imprinting object, and studies were made for birds aged 18, 32 and 48 hours. Compared with controls (no shocks) of the same age, the shocked birds followed nearly twice as far in the given time at 18 hours; but the difference, while always in favour of the 'shocked' birds, declined progressively at the later ages. In a second experiment, four different groups of birds underwent different conditions at the three age levels of 14, 18 and 32 hours. The conditions were: controls, 27 'light' shocks (1 mA for 5 seconds), 27 'heavy' shocks (3 mA for 5 seconds) and 11 'heavy' shocks. Those receiving 27 'light' or 11 'heavy' shocks were ahead of controls at 14 and 18 hours of age, and those receiving 11 'heavy' shocks were slightly the better. At 32 hours of age, controls (no shocks) were slightly ahead. At 14 and 18 hours, members of groups receiving 27 'heavy' shocks performed worst of all. At all ages, those receiving shocks were more active and vocal; but at the younger ages, the activity was directed towards the imprinting object. The obvious conclusion from this study is that a moderate amount of shock is conducive to better following, but only up to the age of 18 hours.

In a later experiment, Fischer et al. (1965) investigated the effect of electro-convulsive shock through the crown of the head upon the responses of chicks which were already well imprinted upon a red, octagonal object equipped with a speaker and heating element. Electro-convulsive shock has been shown to impair retention in rats, and the experimenters explored the effects in chickens by using shocks which were strong enough to produce convulsions. These shocks were administered outside the original training run, but for retention tests the animals were returned to the original run. In the crucial following and discrimination tests, a high correlation was recorded between following and discrimination. One electrically induced convulsion did not affect following, but a series of nine such treatments did. The authors see no reason why such effects upon imprinting should not be regarded as comparable with those found to apply in the extensive literature on learning to discriminate and avoid particular stimuli and patterns of stimuli. They regard imprinting as the conditioning of an innate social response to a specific stimulus object by means of repeated social reinforcement.

The determination of the differences between imprinting and other types of learning, if they do exist, is difficult,

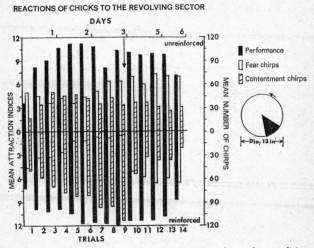

Fig. 3. *Chicks were randomly allotted to either condition, approach to the revolving sector with the reinforcement of food and water available, or not. The reinforced group (lower half of graph) approach better, give more content- ment chirps and fewer fear chirps. Note the gradual change when after day 3 the reinforcement is withdrawn. No trials were held on day 4 and two on day 6.*

particularly since, as Smith and Harding (unpublished) have shown, responses to various kinds of intermittent visual stimuli, which will take place perfectly well without any external reinforcement, can be made slightly better by such rewards or reinforcement (See Fig. 3). Several of the above-mentioned studies, however, have indicated that responsive-ness and the effect of certain conditions are related to the age of the young bird, and we will therefore turn now to the consideration of this factor.

THE CRITICAL OR OPTIMAL PERIOD

The concept of a critical period during which particular responses can be acquired, and beyond which the acquisition is difficult or impossible, has not been confined to the behaviour of birds. It was directly implicit in all the Freudian literature on human infantile attachments and, as Thorpe (1963) has pointed out, frequently arises in the development of instincts and in the acquisition of song patterns by chaffinches. Scott and Marston (1950), Scott (1962) and Deneberg (1964) have argued for the existence of several different critical periods, depending on the nature of the response to be acquired. Schutz (1963a, b, 1965a), for example, has produced evidence that the critical period for following and social attachments in Mallards is different from that for sexual attachments. Again, for many activities there is a close association between what has been regarded as maturation and the critical period. Riesen's apes (1950), deprived of precise visual and tactile experience in the early months of life, never attained normal powers of visual discrimination. Padilla (1935) has also reported that chicks reared in darkness and fed from a small spoon for the first two weeks after hatching never developed the pecking response and starved to death in cages with abundant food and grit.

Many of the studies of critical or sensitive periods have been carried out with domestic species and, to attain greater accuracy in certain phases of the work, in laboratories. These facts may have introduced sources of variability. Klopfer (1956) has suggested that for domestic ducks and geese imprinting could be highly maladaptive because of the possibility of imprinting on the wrong object. In the more dispersed conditions in the wild it is adaptive. The factual evidence is that hybridisation is rare in birds. Klopfer suggests that precise imprinting within consistent critical periods could only be maintained in the context of strong selective pressure and that the comparative safety and inbreeding, associated with domestication, has resulted in greater variability and loss of precision in many aspects of imprinting. Again, it should be stressed that accurate psychometric scaling of the intrinsic strength of attraction of the many stimulus conditions used in experiments has not been done, and variations in reported results could be expected for this reason alone.

However, in an actual experiment with wild and semi-wild Mallard ducklings and Peking ducklings (the domestic form of the Mallard), Gottlieb (1961b) found no marked and significant differences in following silent or sounding models; but the domesticated Peking ducklings showed by far the least avoidance behaviour. This could reflect a long history of domestication and relaxation of selective pressure; but fear in any form is thought by many observers to be only one of the factors relevant to responsiveness. Stated broadly, opinion on the determinants of the length of the critical period involve the following possibilities:

(i) The following response appears and declines as a naturally occurring and internally determined reaction, a view expressed by Lorenz (1935) and Fabricius (1951a).

(ii) While the occurrence may arise as above, the termination of the period is brought about by the development of fear early in the life of the bird.

(iii) There is a 'mixed' position, in which the length of the period is regarded as the resultant with which many variables such as age, previous experience of the bird, the onset of fear and the strength of the stimulus are associated.

The subsequent treatment will review evidence relevant to these positions.

SOME POSSIBLE INTERNAL DETERMINANTS

Gray (1962), working with White Leghorn chicks, has drawn attention to a possible diurnal rhythm. His subjects were hatched and maintained in isolation. Chicks in a separate group were tested individually at successive three-hour intervals on each of the first four days. The chick was placed in a central compartment, with a White Leghorn hen in the

next compartment on one side and an age-mate in a corresponding enclosure on the other. A significant and increasing
preference for the hen, reaching a maximum around midnight
and which then reversed in all cases in favour of the age-mate,
was claimed. Response to the hen declined slowly over four
days, but there were no significant differences between days.
Gray suggested that rhythms of this kind should be considered
when estimating critical periods. In a later experiment (Gray
et al., 1964), attention was confined to the first day with
exposures of 15 seconds before each preference test at 3, 9,
15 and 24 hours of age. A diurnal rhythm was again apparent
and also an increasing preference for the age-mate, as the age
increased. Such rhythms certainly are relevant; but the use of
moving animals of different sizes introduces a number of
perceptual variables which are, even with the greatest care,
difficult to control.

Sackett (1963), taking a cue from the work of Maturna *et al.*
(1960) on the tectal lobes and optic nerve of the frog, suggests
that maturation of the retina is the key to the critical period.
In the Frog (*Rana pipiens*) five classes of ganglion cells were
distinguished which appear to mediate such specific information as sustained edge detection, convex edge detection,
detection of contrast and of dimming and darkness. These cells
are claimed to mature at different rates and become operative
at different times. Such a theory might be relevant to the onset
of the critical period, but not to its termination.

Moltz and Rosenblum (1958a) attempted to analyse the
response of Peking ducklings into separate components
according to the age of the chicks. One test trial was held on
each of the first 15 days with a silent model which moved for
10 minutes, paused for 5 minutes, and moved for a further
10 minutes. By carefully noting the times when the chick was
within 12 inches behind or 6 inches to one side of the model,
an accumulation of times gave a score for the moving object
and a 'stationary score'. The peak for the moving score was
five to six days, for the stationary score around three to four
days, and, unlike the 'moving score' which declined after
seven days, was better sustained but with a dramatic fall to

zero at 15 days. Brown (1964) was also interested in the stimulus properties of motionless objects and worked with selected Silver Oklabar chicks (a broiler breed developed in Oklahoma). The chicks were individually housed in boxes with coloured interiors. A different food-box with a coloured interior was presented on each of the first five days. On the sixth day, a choice of boxes in the five different colours was offered. The chicks tended to choose the colours most recently presented. In a second experiment, five groups of birds were presented with a coloured box on only one day. Neutral grey boxes were offered on the other four days. Evidence of learning was only apparent from the fifth day. In a third experiment, chicks were deprived of food for the first three days and subsequently treated as in the first experiment. Again, in the choice test the chicks tended to choose the colours encountered on the fourth and fifth days, post-hatch.

The possibility of different sensitive or critical periods for different types of motion, for colour and conformation of the stimulus object is raised by the foregoing experiments, but in the absence of further rigorous experimentation, can only remain a possibility. A potentially important factor in Brown's experiments was habituation. This may have offset fear of boxes encountered on the later days and thus influenced responses to the boxes, which were not encountered as novel stimuli in the choice situation.

FEAR AND THE CRITICAL PERIOD

Hebb (1946) submits that the cause of fear in any animal is the impression of discrepancy or cleavage between former perceptions of an object or situation and the present one, i.e. 'fear occurs when an object is seen which is like familiar objects in enough respects to arouse habitual processes of perception but in other respects arouses incompatible processes'. Many observations of young birds are consistent with this view, and it may be that the common observation that few birds display fear in early life is due to the simple fact that until the bird has had time to build some stable impressions of and reactions to the environment, no sense of discrepancy can arise. The consistent finding from Schaller and Emlen's extensive tests (1700) on nearly 400 birds of 15 species was that the essential factor in eliciting avoidance of an object was strangeness. A number of studies provide elaboration of this view and information as to timing.

Phillips and Siegel (1966) worked with domestic chicks from matings of F.6 generation birds in lines of White Plymouth Rocks, selected for high and low body weight. Birds ranging in age from 6 to 168 hours, post-hatch, were tested once only for their reaction to the sound of an electric door-bell placed in a small cubicle to which they were habituated for 60 seconds. They were then closely observed for three minutes, and records were made of postural responses, mobility, cheeping, defecation and response to a hand thrust at them at the end of the period. Newly hatched chicks showed little response to the sudden loud noise; but response rose to a peak after two days, thereafter falling but maintaining a high level. The genetic lines differed significantly; but although the responses were often higher for isolates, there were no statistically significant differences between birds housed socially and those in isolation.

A different approach to the study of fear is that of Ratner and Thompson (1960). In moments of great stress, chicks crouch in a so-called 'immobility' posture. This can be induced by holding the chick down for about 10 to 15 seconds. In a study of over 200 White Leghorn chicks and 83 pure-bred male Cobb chicks, the immobility reaction was found to be virtually absent before the age of 7 to 10 days; but thereafter, once induced, it was maintained for the arbitrary test period of 12 minutes adopted in the study until the birds were 59 days of age. Salzen (1963a) was able to promote the immobility reaction by holding the (Brown Leghorn × Light Sussex) chick on its back for 15 seconds. During this time, struggling usually ceased and restraint became unnecessary. He confirmed Ratner and Thompson's finding that the reaction does not appear until the age of seven or eight days and is very much more likely to occur in socially housed than in isolated chicks. He also found that in tests at the age of eight days and at 14 to 16 days, the reaction was significantly *less* likely to occur in socially housed chicks if they were tested in the presence of other chicks. Since the isolates tended to show no reaction at all and the socially housed chicks showed reaction mainly when tested alone, Salzen attached considerable importance to the loss of stimulation from companions – in short, to the discrepancy in experience and the appearance of a strong fear reaction.

In another series of experiments with isolated and socially housed chicks of the same breed, Salzen found further evidence for the same basic conclusion. Fear of a strange static environment, i.e. the empty test run, was shown by all chicks which had had the time to become familiar with another environment, while fear of the strange moving object (the imprinting object) was shown only by birds that had had 24 hours experience of other chicks, or in Salzen's phrase, a 'neural organisation' or an impression of movement discrepant from the novel object.

A similar view arises from an experiment by Sluckin and Salzen (1961). They erected a small overhead circular railway from which objects could be suspended, and in one corner of the enclosure provided a small covered 'hover' where food and water were always available. The chicks were soon following the model, but as time went on they would follow sporadically and spend more time in the hover. A sudden loud noise or the appearance of a strange object, however, would very often be followed by 'distress' cheeping and a rapid resumption of following. A related study is that of Moltz *et al.* (1959), who showed that, of birds living in visual isolation, and which had shown a strong following response to a green moving object, those which received shocks inside the run when the imprinting object was removed subsequently followed significantly better than those receiving no shocks and those which received shocks outside the test run. Again, Jaynes (1958b) found that while retention of early imprinting at the age of 30 days improved directly in proportion to time spent in early imprinting sessions, of the more practised (40 minutes training) and thus those retaining most, only 17% showed fear responses. Of the least practised and least successful group (5 minutes training), 83% showed some fear responses.

A sensitive study of the balance between approach and avoidance over the first five days after hatching was provided by Bateson (1964d). Once following began, it tended to increase and the proportion of each minute of the test spent in avoiding tended to decrease. The two indices of fear, strength of avoidance and persistence of avoidance, were positively and significantly correlated, tending to eke out a fundamental picture suggested by other studies that, after the first few days, approaches and following take place in a context of which fear is a part. Hess and Schaefer (1959), for example, found with Leghorn chicks that approach and fixation were at a maximum by the age of eight hours when using a suspended model of a male Mallard equipped with a heater and a speaker. However, approach and fixation had declined to zero at 21 hours and between 29 and 32 hours, respectively. Contentment chirps declined from a maximum at 8 hours to zero at 32 hours, while distress began at 9 to 12 hours and increased into the second day. In a study with naïve Mallard ducklings, Boyd and Fabricius (1965) found that 46% of the birds reacted to silent moving objects by avoidance at 10 to 20 hours, the percentage increasing to 100 % by 240 hours. Of the 58 % which began to follow within the period 10 to 20 hours of age, only 17% were following by 240 hours, when testing ceased.

The evidence to date would appear to indicate that, with possible variations between different species of birds, fear emerges after an appreciable interval from hatching and is clearly a potent contributing factor in many responses, including those associated with imprinting. Moltz and Stettner (1961), by a simple and instructive experiment, have suggested the nature of this context. The imprinting object was a green cardboard box suspended from a rotating, endless belt. Recently hatched Peking ducklings were divided into two major groups. Those in group 1 were fitted with small latex hoods which permitted light to enter but no precise patterned vision. Group 2, the controls, wore similar hoods, but tiny holes made patterned vision possible. Each group was further

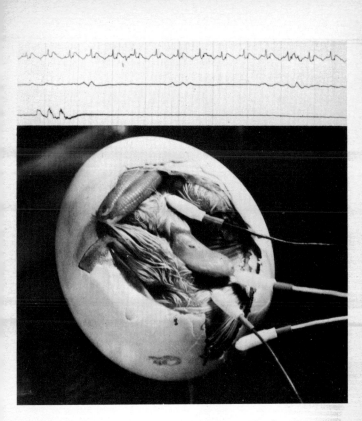

Plate I. *Method of recording from the duck embryo. The fine electrodes are inserted at the points shown, and data recorded. The top line is a recording of heart-beat, the middle line records bill-clapping, and the third line indicates the small burst of vocalisation. The foetus at this stage can vocalise without making overt bill movements.*

Plate II (a). *The Wood Duckling* (circled) *drops from the nesting box in response to the mother's call. The evidence suggests that the Wood Ducklings, after hatching, imprint readily upon sounds from the mother and very poorly, if at all, on visual impressions.*

Plate II (b). *The Wood Duck, with her brood partially assembled on the water, attacks and drives away an intruding Mallard.*

Plate III (a). *The approach of newly-born lambs to the teat is uncertain and subject to much trial and error. The picture shows a lamb, born half an hour previously, butting the folds of a corn sack while the ewe nuzzles and licks the small body, despite the heavy rain. The instinct in the young lamb appears to be to insert the head under any projecting or overhanging surface at about the height of its shoulder. Eventually, and probably with olfactory cues, the teat is found.*

Plate III (b). *A variety of wrong orientations are always observed. Normally the teat is found within half an hour from the time the lamb comes to its feet, i.e. within the first hour of life.*

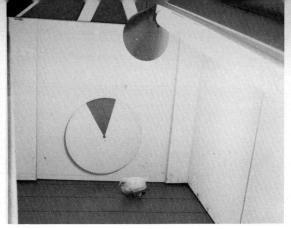

Plate IV. *A young chicken which has just approached the rotating sector from the other end of a prepared run, the floor of which is marked in stages to help in measuring the distance and speed of approach. The chicks will very often remain near the slowly rotating disc, pecking in the vicinity and giving contentment chirps.*

Plate V. *The young ape on the surrogate mother, which consists of a metal frame similar to the one on the left but covered with thick towelling.*

subdivided into those exposed to the box at the age of 12, 24, 48 and 72 hours, post-hatch. Hoods were removed just before the crucial trials. Following responses were significantly in favour of the experimental group at 24 and 48 hours (See Fig. 4). Avoidance responses in the first five minutes were very significantly greater among the controls at 24 hours and after. One obvious implication is that the more inexperienced or perceptually naïve the bird is, the less likely it is to show fear

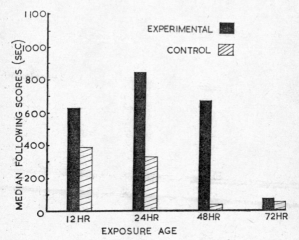

Fig. 4. *Median following scores obtained by experimental and control groups for different groups exposed at various ages. Note the very poor response for both groups at the age of 72 hours. (After Moltz and Stettner, 1961. By kind permission of the authors and of the editor of* Journal of Comparative and Physiological Psychology.)

responses and the more likely it is to follow. The performance of both groups at 72 hours, however, would suggest that processes within the bird, independent of experience, are beginning to operate by the third day. In a later experiment, Moltz *et al.* (1962) showed that denial of patterned vision to one eye during training trials did not result in any significant decline in following when the same eye was uncovered and the other covered with the latex hood.

APPROXIMATE ESTIMATES OF THE TIMING OF THE CRITICAL PERIOD

Since a great variety of experimental procedures and several different species have been used, it is impossible to combine the findings of different studies. The crude facts seem to be, however, that if approach or following has not been induced by the second or third day of age, it becomes increasingly more difficult to achieve. Latent imprinting is possible, as Jaynes (1957) has pointed out and as Salzen and Sluckin (1959) have confirmed, in the sense that birds apparently unresponsive in trials on the second or third day later respond better than naïve birds; but in general it may be stated that, for any given stimulus situation, longer training times must be used as the age increases. Testing 500 Rhode Island Red chicks, Salzen and Sluckin (1959) found that 50% of the birds responded to 10 movements of the box, and 80% to 50 movements, on the first day. No bird in this study responded after first seeing the box five days after hatching, and differences between those given 10 and 50 movements of the box were not significant after day 3. Sluckin (1962) has subsequently shown, however, that one to four hours training given on the eighth and ninth days, post-hatch, can mediate effective discrimination at the age of 15 days.

With Mallard ducklings, Ramsay and Hess (1954) and Hess in several studies suggest an optimum responsiveness in the neighbourhood of 16 hours. Fabricius (1955) puts the peak for Mallards a little later, in the neighbourhood of 25 to 30 hours, and Weidmann (1958) has indicated 5 to 40 hours as the probable limits of the Mallard's responsiveness. Alley and Boyd (1950) suggest the first eight hours for Coots. Polt and Hess (1966), experimenting with social and isolate conditions, incline to a period near 16 hours for Vantress Broiler chicks and possibly a little later for those socially housed.

However, as frequently emphasised, variations in housing, prior stimulation and the strength of the stimulus can affect response. Smith and Nott (in press) have shown that using a particularly strong combination of visual and auditory stimuli, a 98% response can be evoked from a chick reared socially and first exposed to the stimulus at a full 10 days, post-hatch. This response was maintained with tests on only alternate days until the bird was 29 days of age, when the tests were concluded.

In general, the foregoing evidence would tend to support the 'mixed' hypothesis, namely that the length of the critical period is a function of several factors, including developmental processes within the bird with which fear is associated, maturing locomotion, experience, and the nature and strength of the stimulus object or pattern to which the bird is exposed.

IMPRINTING AND SUBSEQUENT REFINEMENT

Lorenz (1935, 1937) draws attention to the range of attachments which may be subsumed under the title of imprinting. At one extreme, there is the type where the young bird would appear to have some innate 'schema' or image of its parents and will attach itself to an adult of its own species and no other. Drawing upon a concept from embryology where each cell of a developing organism appears to fulfil a specific function at an appropriate time, Lorenz describes this type of attachment as the 'mosaic' type of imprinting and cites a newly hatched Curlew (*Numenius arquata*) or a Godwit (*Limosa limosa*) which will flee at the sight of a human being. Very different is the behaviour of the Greylag gosling (*Anser anser*) immediately after hatching. In Heinroth's (1911) observation, it must not be allowed to see a human being on emerging from the incubator if it is to follow and become attached to its parents. This modifiable response corresponds to the induction of some cells of the embryo by their immediate cellular environment into the fulfilment of a specific function. To this adaptable type of imprinting response Lorenz applies the term 'regulative', and obviously, as previous chapters have shown, this form lends itself readily to experimental study. Indeed, its very adaptability has been associated with some bizarre results.

The author has several times been able to induce avid

following to a red box in domestic ducklings (Khaki Camp-bells), and after several training trials with this object for eight consecutive days and with virtually a maximum response, the birds transferred similar rapid approach to a flashing light, a rotating black and white disc and the author himself. Steven (1955) has reported an instance of a Lesser White-fronted gosling (*Anser erythropus*) which had been observed as part of a flock of six adults and ten goslings over a period of four days before capture. The bird was thus well imprinted on adults of its own kind. On the fifth day of captivity it ap-proached to an imitation 'gek gek' call, and on the sixth day it followed Steven persistently, and then other members of his party. Fabricius and Boyd (1953) have also reported that Mallard ducklings which had followed their mother for 36 hours could be induced to follow a balloon. Lorenz (1937) cites the case of a Budgerigar (*Melopsittacus undulatus*), reared in isolation, which transferred its social reactions to a blue and white celluloid ball. It preened the non-existent feathers of the ball and presented its own neck for preening. A young Jackdaw, reared in isolation, treated human beings as parents, used hooded crows as flight companions, and led and fed a baby jackdaw in the normal manner of a parent. Räber (1948) describes a hand-reared cock Turkey (*Meleagris*) which courted men, attacked women or men with brief-cases or flapping scarves, and repeatedly copulated with a variety of objects the size of a Turkey hen. It is possible, however, that some perceptual feature in each of these situations resembled the sign stimulus appropriate to each of the innate releasing mechanisms mediating these several activities. On the other hand, the innate tendency of the Greylag goose to follow a moving object could be expressed in being imprinted on a man whom it followed while he walked and swam, but was trans-ferred to other Greylags as soon as they took wing.

Yet, apart from such inappropriate developments, there are many observations where processes akin to imprinting and not involving filial responses are of obvious use to the bird. Swanberg (1951) has shown that it takes the Thick-billed Nutcracker (*Nucifraga caryocatactes caryocatactes*) only three minutes to hide a heap of nuts in the ground, but the bird can find the cache several months later, even when covered with snow, and Klopfer (1965b) has produced some interesting evidence that the tropical Blue Tanager (*Thraupis cana*) can acquire a bias towards a particular type of foliage.

It should be remembered that many, though not all, abnormal sexual attachments represent a preference for the particular object, not a rigid response, exclusive of other possibilities. Schein (1963) has shown that his White Holland turkeys, imprinted on human beings in their first days, preferred five years later to address their sexual advances to human beings, but if none were available, they successfully fertilised turkey hens. Craig, too, in 1914, found that his Ring Doves, while they gave up their attachment to human beings with difficulty, did eventually associate with their own species.

Two facts emerge from these observations on the regulative type of imprinting: first, that the attachments can be strong and lasting, and, secondly, that since over a period of time modification or transference of a response is involved, some features of learning may be relevant.

There can be little doubt that the activity of following and the proximity to the stimulus object or source is in some way satisfying or rewarding to the bird. There is clear evidence with precocial birds that the process is closely associated with emotional activity. Proximity to the stimulus is associated with contentment or pleasure chirps, distance or removal of the object with marked distress calling. In some cases this satisfying emotional attachment is achieved quickly, in others it is slower, with gradually increasing awareness of perceptual details; but, whatever the method, the significance of the attachment for the bird is such that, like food or warmth, it has many of the characteristics of a need and can be used as the unconditioned stimulus (like the meat powder for Pavlov's dogs) in the acquisition of other responses. James (1959), using flashing light as the unconditioned stimulus, was able to condition approach responses to an adjoining blue doll. Campbell

and Pickleman (1961) have used the imprinting object as a
reward or reinforcement to secure a significant choice of path
by chicks in a 'T' maze. Peterson (1960) arranged that his
Black ducklings (*Anas rubripes tristis*) and Peking ducklings
should press a key to secure the appearance of the object on
which they had previously been imprinted. This reward
mediated some quite complicated learning, in the sense that
the ducklings had to (and some did) learn that every eighth peck
secured the appearance of the object. In another experiment
they learned that if the key was trans-illuminated, reinforcement was contingent on 10 pecks; if darkened, one minute
without pecking was required. If the strength of an imprinting-
type attachment can mediate other attachments and discriminations in this way, the potential loss in social adjustment and
general competence to birds which are prevented from achiev-
ing an attachment, must be considerable.

The process of attachment is possible with varying degrees
of discrimination. Initially, mere movement or intermittent
stimulation is sufficient to ensure approach and following,
and the birds can generalise their response to a range of
objects having the fundamental quality of movement. This is
akin to the phenomenon known in psychological literature as
stimulus generalisation. As the days pass, however, the birds
learn more of the details of the object, as can be shown by the
bird's ability to discriminate between the familiar and the
strange object. In psychological literature this has become
known as perceptual learning. The literature on imprinting
affords illustrations of both. Hinde *et al.* (1956) found with
Moorhens and Coots that once the young birds were following,
they would generalise this response to a wide range of objects,
the Coots even up to the age of 60 days. Jaynes (1958b),
working with New Hampshire Red chicks, used a red cylinder
in 30-minute imprinting sessions on each of the first four days
of life. With an interval of about four minutes, each animal
was then given an opportunity to follow one of five strange
objects. Response to the original red cylinder was not impeded
by the fact of the chick's approach to the new object. Express-
ing the score for following the strange object as a percentage

of those to the original training object, the averages for the four days were 97, 79, 77, 81. The 'generalisation decrement' was found to be a statistically reliable trait of the individual chick. In discrimination tests on the fifth day of life, the strange object was followed 81% as much as the original red cylinder in the first five minutes, but thereafter the chicks tended to spend more time in the vicinity of the original object.

As Cofoid and Honig (1961) point out, however, the objects in the foregoing studies involved several perceptual variables. By using a globe illuminated by light from a tungsten filament lamp via Kodak Wratten filters as the moving, imprinting object, they were able to explore the problem of generalisation with colours of wavelength 470, 486, 501, 520, 535 and 555 mμ. To human observation, these ranged from violet-blue to yellowish-green. The domestic White Rock chicks received 30 minutes with the object at 470 mμ on the first day of life, and 17 minutes on each of the next three days. The object also emitted sound. On days 5 and 6 the object was presented for three minutes in all six wavelengths in random order, the sound being omitted on day 6. The decrement in amount of following was not severe, going down from 180 seconds at 470 mμ to 100 seconds at 550 mμ. On day 6 the following was generally better, which the authors claim indicates that sound was not critical; but in view of other findings on arousal by Pitz and Ross (1961) and Smith and Bird (1963b), the possible contribution of the sound in promoting response could not be ignored.

Evidence for perceptual learning in birds is widespread, and not surprisingly it occurs in the two sensory modalities which they use predominantly – namely, audition and vision. The ability of birds to imitate and acquire sound patterns has been amply demonstrated by Thorpe (1963), Marler (1961) and others. An interesting indication of specificity in visual, perceptual learning is reported by Hess (1950). One group of chicks was reared for seven weeks in a cage illuminated only from above. Another group were reared in a cage to which light came only through the translucent floor. In crucial trials, photographs including corn grains illuminated from above and others from below were shown to the chicks, who reacted selectively and pecked according to their experience. Bateson (1964a) has shown too that birds reared individually from day 2 to day 8 in compartments with vertical black-and-white-striped walls were significantly better than those reared with other patterns in discriminations where panels with black and white striping had to be distinguished from panels with red and yellow horizontal stripes. In another experiment, Bateson (1964e) found, by infra-red recording in the living boxes, that chicks reared in boxes with plain grey walls were much more active over the first seven days of life than those reared within walls painted in black and white vertical stripes but which reflected the same amount of light. This suggests the possibility that in early life the bird tends to seek and perhaps needs varied stimulation. Some indirect support for such an hypothesis may be derived from the studies of learning by Vince (1958, 1960) with a number of species – Greenfinches (*Chloris chloris*), Chaffinches, Canaries and the Great Tit (*Parus major*). Young birds appear to be more active and responsive but inhibition which is relevant in acquiring a discrimination is much more stable in older birds.

From farther afield, interesting evidence of what appears to be perceptual learning is reported by Sladen (1958) of the Adélie Penguins (*Pygoscelis adeliae*). At about the age of four to five weeks the young are left on land in large crèches while both parents forage in the sea for food. It was noted that, on return, the parent walked determinedly through the crèche, all the young watching intently. Recognition was sometimes marked by loud, mutual display. In the 1948–49 Antarctic summer, colour rings were placed around the flippers of chicks of marked parents before the crèche stage. Out of a total of 71 observations, only twice were parents found to be feeding chicks which were not their own. In both cases these were chicks fed in addition to their own.

Now, such instances of perceptual learning by birds over a period of time are more in the nature of extended 'regulative' imprinting than the precise 'mosaic' type, where almost instantaneously, and within a very brief period in early life, lasting attachments are formed to the 'schema' of the parents and to this alone. Between the two are such types illustrated by Gottlieb (1965b) and Klopfer (1959a), where naïve ducklings of different species were found to respond to the calls of more than one species but displayed a preference for the calls of their own. There is evidence, as Bacon *et al.* (1962) have shown, that birds can learn quite complicated discriminations if given sufficient cues, such as colour, form and area, and sufficient time; and to the extent that the hypothetical 'schema' is not completely adequate, specific attachments in some species would appear to depend very significantly on perceptual learning. Cases of imprinting in altricial birds (those helpless for some time after birth and in consequence usually nidicolous, i.e. remaining in the nest) are known. Klinghammer and Hess (1964) have reported evidence of imprinting on the squabs of Blond Ring Doves (*Streptopelia risoria*) which remain in the nest for about 14 days and must be fed by their parents for at least 21 days. They estimate the optimum time for imprinting to be at seven to nine days. Immelmann too (1967), by interchanging eggs between clutches of the grass finches, Zebra Finch (*Taeniopygia guttata castanotis*), Bengalese Finch (*Lochura striata f. domesticata*) and the African Silverbill, (*Euodice cantans*), allowing the young to be raised by the foster parents and then isolating the young when they had reached independence, found very convincing evidence of social and sexual imprinting. All males tested to date significantly preferred females of the foster species or models thereof. They would pair with females of their own species *faute de mieux*, but the preference for the foster species still remained. In some birds the acquired preference has lasted five years. Immelmann thinks that imprinting on the birds' own species is always stronger and less easy to reverse than imprinting on the foster species. This would appear to indicate that something in the nature of an innate 'schema' or bias may exist; but it can definitely be overcome by experience with, and apparently learning of, the perceptual characteristics of the foster species.

Kovach *et al.* (1966) have investigated the long-range effects of early perceptual learning of an artificial feature, the appearance of a flickering patch of light which the individually housed White Cornish chicks first encountered at the age of 14 to 18 hours for 30 minutes and again for 3 hours on the second day. The chicks were divided into 'approachers' and 'non-approachers' and these groups, with controls, were placed in a common brooder at 48 hours. One month later, crucial learning tests were conducted in a standard Yerkes alley, discrimination procedure with random location of stimuli and food rewards. The alternative stimulus to the flickering light (original imprinting stimulus) was a stable light. The 'approachers' were significantly better than the 'non-approachers' or controls (which did not differ significantly) in learning to discriminate with the aid of reward; but in more complicated tasks of learning to reverse response to the alternative stimulus, the 'approachers' were slower at first in reversing their responses, although they soon caught up.

Kovach, Fabricius and Fält go so far in discussing their results as to claim that 'it is possible that the long-range effects of imprinting are based neither on an irreversible attachment to the imprinting stimulus nor a unique formation of social bond (Scott, 1962), but on an acquisition process comparable to perceptual learning'. But this view probably applies more appropriately to those species in which any form of innate endowment or 'schema' is less than precise or incomplete and thus less prescriptive. The capacity for perceptual learning in most birds is such that if there exists an innate tendency to approach anything involving movement, the close proximity can ensure the linking of the response to a stimulus object in which the bird becomes aware of an increasing number of details as time goes on, and thus becomes more capable of discrimination between familiar and strange objects. The difference between the most rapid and perfect example of imprinting and the many practice trials necessary to imprint an unresponsive member of a domestic species seems to be one of degree.

To the extent that some contribution of effective attachment and power to discriminate must come via learning, it is thus reasonable to expect that some combinations of stimuli and some objects would be more suitable than others. This has been abundantly demonstrated by Fabricius (1951b), Smith (1960), Smith and Hoyes (1961), Smith (1962), Smith and Bird (1964b) and others. Yet the optimum conformation of the imprinting object could perhaps be further defined. Guhl and Ortman (1953) have moved in this direction, though only indirectly, since they were studying peck orders in small flocks of domestic fowl at the age of five months. Their method consisted in adding different amounts of material and colours to the birds. Features of the head and neck were found to be more influential in producing loss of recognition than changes in the trunk. A large comb appears to be an advantage in initial encounters. Intense colour changes on white individuals also produced more loss of recognition than the application of shades or tints. Schein and Hale (1959) too found that the head seemed by far the most important in attracting precocious sexual responses from turkey poults. Carbaugh *et al.* (1962), while they found the body of their taxidermic models of hens necessary for releasing complete sexual responses in adult White Leghorn males, noted the importance of the head in orientating and releasing sexual behaviour. The presence or absence of the tail appeared to have little effect, except that when present the prone position of the tail tended to raise the level of sexual behaviour. Not inconsistently Fisher and Hale (1956) found, by using a variety of models both female and male, that the sexual response of their New Hampshire and Barred Plymouth Rocks males was not related to the apparent sex of the model, but definitely influenced by its posture. All models elicited sexual responses; but crouched models were the most effective.

Again, Klopfer and Hailman (1964b) and Klopfer (1965a) have reported that Vantress Cross chicks and Mallard duck-lings which were following a plain model of a mallard decoy, chose to follow a more brightly striped model when offered a simultaneous choice. It appears, therefore, that in the acquire-ment of discrimination and preferences, some features are intrinsically more attractive to birds and perhaps also easier to learn.

5. Later Social and Sexual Aspects of Imprinting

In considering the long-range effects of early attachments, it is important to appreciate how complicated, in the case of some species, the social context of adult behaviour can be. In flocks of domestic fowl, for example, there is a definite pecking hierarchy, the less dominant bird being pecked by the other. This general type of organisation is not limited to birds. The less dominant baboon will groom another, higher in the social order. Geist (1966) has reported too that among the rams of a flock of Bighorn Sheep (*Ovis canadensis canadensis*), the more dominant male kicks the less dominant and the chief determinant of position in the hierarchy is the size of the horns. In a flock of domestic fowl, Marks *et al.* (1960) showed that dubbing of comb and wattles lowered the rank order of the birds. McBride (1964) has also indicated a dominance order between strains when they occupy the same terrain. In another study of a population of feral fowls on an island off the Queensland coast and subsequently continued on the mainland, McBride (1967) was able to demonstrate some remarkable spatial relationships maintained between different grades of the social order. A dominant male inhibited all aggressive behaviour among females within a radius of 8 to 10 ft, and among subordinate males within 15 to 20 ft. Broody hens inhibited aggressive behaviour among chicks within 1·5 and 2 ft, and displayed when approached to within 15 to 20 ft by other fowl.

Lill and Wood-Gush (1965) have drawn attention to the importance of the waltz and the rear approach by Brown Leghorn cocks in evoking favourable responses from the hens. Other studies by Wood-Gush (1956, 1958) have indicated among Brown Leghorn cocks what might be regarded as a language of behavioural signs or gestures. Among the agonistic (associated with fighting) signs are strutting, the high-stepping advance, fighting stance and retreating. Waltzing, wing flapping, titbitting (pecking and scratching the ground), wing flapping and feather ruffling are included in the courtship displays. Thwarting of sexual activity appeared to promote display, and cocks displayed more on entering strange pens. Wood-Gush inclines to the view that agonistic displays by the cock are more likely to occur when the bird is in a state of conflict between aggression and retreat. He found a low correlation between aggressiveness and sexual activity. Success in fighting was significantly correlated with measures of aggression, but not with sexual activity. Again, from his close analysis of the behaviour of 22 cockerels, he found no correlation between sexual activity and the pecking order. The importance of a normal social life within the flock in enabling the growing bird to learn the appropriate use of social gestures has been effectively demonstrated by Kruijt (1962, 1964) in extensive studies of the Burmese Red Jungle Fowl (*Gallus gallus spadiceus*). Male chicks kept in visual isolation from other chicks and fowls, when introduced to females at 9 to 16 months of age, while fully capable of ejaculation, were in many cases socially and sexually inept. They were incapable of integrating the opposing tendencies of aggression and escape, and reacted excessively, both with aggression and escape, and even to innocuous stimuli such as a sparrow flitting into or outside the cage. Instead of the customary dignified waltz and gradual courting, their approach to the hens was usually inept and violent. Waltzing might appear but it was unrefined, being too sustained and not adapted to the reactions of the female, who was often viciously attacked and mounted the wrong way round. The denial of early imprinting and social experience had in fact produced a socially inept bird.

Kruijt's study isolated the jungle fowl for at least nine

months. Baron and Kish (1960) reared groups of White Rock chicks for the first four weeks of life in conditions of complete social isolation, in pairs, or in a flock. From the age of 5 to 10 weeks all the birds were reared in identical flock conditions. Tested at the end of the fourth week for the time spent near a stimulus bird of the same age, the socially reared chicks and pairs were found to be more sociable than the isolates. In tests at the end of the tenth week, however, the former 'isolates' recorded times between the other two groups, suggesting that the experience of the last six weeks had compensated for early experience. In a later study, Baron *et al.* (1962) used three groups of chicks; namely, those submitted to social conditions for the first 10 weeks of life (S); another group which had social conditions for the first week and isolation for 9 weeks (S-1); and a third group which was isolated for the first week and given social conditions for 9 weeks (1-S). Tests of response to a bird of the same age in a display compartment were conducted at 5 and 10 weeks. In terms of the percentage of time spent near the stimulus, there were virtually no differences between the (S) and (1-S) groups at five weeks; but time scores for the (S-1) were much lower, and the birds were very significantly more emotional. At 10 weeks the time scores were higher for the (S) group, while both experimental groups (1-S) and (S-1) were appreciably lower. The activity scores of these groups, however, were significantly higher than the socials. Again, over the longer period the experience of the first week appears to have been offset. Waller and Waller (1963) used a shorter period, viz. 14 days, but used pairs and isolated Peking ducklings. One group had no exposure to a moving green cube (nil group), another had 15 minutes exposure at age 10 to 18 hours and 24 hours later (imprint group), and the third group had 15 minutes exposure at the age of 80 hours and again 24 hours later (late group). At the age of 14 days preference tests, with cube and a model of a Peking duck, and flocking tests were conducted. In discrimination, all 'imprint' birds were better as a group at the second exposure to the choice situation than all 'late' birds, but there were no significant differences, for each condition, between pairs and isolates. In flocking, pairs tended to be better than isolates, but outstanding were the isolates of the 'imprint' group. The 'imprint' group, of course, had their experience of the object at what would be regarded as a more sensitive period than the 'late' group and, in consequence, might be regarded as probably better imprinted. Taylor and Sluckin (1964) have confirmed a significant relationship between early imprinting and later flocking in domestic chicks, and it would appear that Waller and Waller had allowed sufficient time for a following response to the green cube to develop up to a point where it was not too exclusive and could be generalised.

Another aspect of communication in the social life of birds is illustrated in the sensitive studies of Würdiger (1967) with small flocks of Bar-headed Geese (*Anser indicus*). By recording and sound spectrographs, she has identified at least six categories in the sounds made by young goslings on their first day of life; these categories are designated: distress calls, lament calls, warning calls, contact calls, greeting calls and sleeping calls. The basic form of the calls remains fairly constant over the first few weeks, although the pitch deepens and the calls become generally stronger. At about the age of seven weeks the distress calls differentiate into the lament call and the distance call. The juvenile contact calls become the adult contact and movement calls, which enable the geese to keep contact and formation when moving and when flying at night. Greeting calls appear to be an intensive form of contact calls and eventually develop into the triumph ceremony. Würdiger relates the attractive story that geese with which she has worked for some time will give the warning call when she herself is exposed to a predatory bird. Again Marler, (1956) has indicated a consistent system of calls or a 'language' among chaffinches. There are, too, the many ritualised preening displays, ritualised drinking and the incitement by the female of the chosen male, which are to be observed among waterfowl, and serve as a form of communication highly relevant and perhaps necessary for successful mate selection and effective reproduction of stable families. Johnsgard (1960, 1965) illustrates many homologies among most of the Anatidae.

Again, there is evidence from the studies of Turner (1965) and Tolman and Wilson (1965) that, provided there is free interaction between members of the flock, there are possibilities for social facilitation and interaction in activities such as feeding. Nottebohm (1967) has also demonstrated that deaf female Ring Doves (*Streptopelia risoria*) are retarded in ovulation: although they hatched chicks, these were not of normal weight and were frequently deserted. Auditory stimulation from the sounds of the flock and the food-begging calls of the squabs appear to be associated with normal ovulation and successful reproduction. Furthermore, Siegel and Siegel (1961), have shown that male chickens placed as a minority among a pen of strangers had significantly heavier left adrenal glands than those remaining among their original flock. Males maintained in groups showed very significant increases in the weights of both adrenals as compared with those housed individually.

There are thus grounds for believing that a complex social life, marked by intense and intimate relationships and requiring appropriate responses to specific gestures, exists for many birds. It is therefore not surprising that, due to accidents, the normal sequence of sexual life is sometimes not achieved.

PRECOCIOUS SEXUAL BEHAVIOUR

Observation of many young animals will often reveal facets of behaviour which are part of the sequence of movements of sexual copulation. Andrew (1966a) has shown that young chicks of a special strain (Hall Sexlink Cross – a first generation from a Rhode Island Red male line and females of a Barred Plymouth Rock line) can be induced to mount the hand of the experimenter if it is repeatedly moved, palm downwards, towards the chick at about the level of its head. With training sessions beginning at the age of 12 ± 4 hours and repeated at intervals of 12 hours, a full pattern of copulation with treading and pelvic thrusts could be obtained in some cases on the second day of life. Similar responses could be obtained from chicks exposed to the movement of other chicks and living in isolated and social conditions. Over the first 16 days of life between 20 and 30% of males copulated, and females occasionally. From the Reeves Pheasant (*Syrmaticus reevesi*) and the Ringneck Pheasant (*Phasianus colchicus*) similar responses were obtained, but not from Quail (*Coturnix coturnix*) and the two species of ducks tested, domestic Muscovy and Mallards. Three female Guinea Fowl (*Numida meleagris*) did not reveal any copulatory patterns, but they indulged in titbitting, which is often a phase of the sexual approaches of the domestic cock.

In a further study with chicks of the Hall Sexlink cross, Andrew (1966b) investigated the possibility that the much studied approach response in chicks might be associated in some way with motivation to copulate. He found no significant differences between carefully isolated males and females in approach to an illuminated and revolving white block in first tests at 24, 48 and 72 hours, and for the first tests at the age of eight days. However, there was some decrease in delay (latency) of response for males treated with testosterone oenanthate as compared with females similarly treated, in tests at 72 hours. The difference approached but did not attain significance at the 5% level of confidence. Andrew nevertheless concluded that 'so small an effect would suggest the appearance of occasional copulation attempts rather than the increased activity of a mechanism important in ordinary following'. At the same time it should be noted that injections of testosterone compounds have been shown to accelerate appearance of several aspects of sexual maturity. Andrew (1963) found an associated increase in the strength and maturity of the chicks calls. Again, in 1964, Andrew demonstrated that chicks, maintained in visual isolation and given daily injections of 0·01 c^3 per 20 gm of body weight of a solution of 25 mg testosterone propionate in oil from the third day, behaved differently from controls. From the third day they pecked and pressed against the imprinting object more intensively, and from day 5 began mounting the test object with significantly greater frequency than did the controls. The difference was observed up to day 45, when observations ceased. None of the controls gave a waltzing display before the object, but one of the injected birds began on day 11 and others on day 14.

It would be tempting to suggest that birds in their first few days possess a complete mechanism capable of mediating the full range of sexual activities with appropriate and additional hormonal activation, but the complete evidence is lacking. In many species, facets of the normal sequence may appear from time to time in early life, sometimes under stress, irritation or stimulation; but this is not a normal pattern, necessarily manifesting sexual motivation. At the same time, sustained and painful or unpleasant experiences associated with one of these partial activities could be important when later the several facets are combined in the full sequence.

Nicolai (1956) may have described a similar partial, though not necessarily decisive phase for later behaviour in the curious betrothal ceremonies between siblings in the same nest of the Bullfinch. In normal adult courtship, the male feeds the female from his crop. Females ready to mate actually search for nesting material, and the showing of nesting material to each other by both parties is normally a sign of acceptance. However, in the nest, young males reveal a great deal of 'female' activity. At this stage both males and females are similar in appearance, and young males carry out much incipient nest building and presentation of nest material to other siblings. These 'betrothals' normally break up even if the betrothed pair are heterosexual. Human attendants, however, can become substitutes for the sibling partner, but again this 'betrothal' is broken if, during the autumn and winter, the birds forms an attachment to a Bullfinch of the opposite sex. Exclusive association with a human being can promote a 'marriage' involving attempts by the bird to feed his abnormal partner.

SOME ABNORMAL ATTACHMENTS

Despite the potentially complex nature of the processes of sexual attachment, many of them display a remarkable durability and this feature is apparent in reports of some abnormal attachments. A young Purple Heron (*Ardea purpurea*) raised in captivity by von Frisch (1957) addressed its courting, nesting and mating behaviour towards its human partner. Strangers were attacked, whereas the familiar man was the object of greeting procedures and even sexual treading upon shoulders. In several respects, the heron was 'married' to the man. Heinroth (1911) reported similar attachments among hand-reared waterfowl, and so did Craig (1914) with doves. It would appear that such attachments are a form of imprinting, and that proximity in early life is the basic cause; but odd cases appear. Goodwin (1948) cites the case of a Turtle Dove (*Streptopelia turtur*), which was raised by its parents till 10 days old, and then by hand with a nest mate which died in January. Many pigeons were flying about in the vicinity. When the dove began to call 'nest' in March, it displayed to every pigeon who came near and, where possible, attempted copulation. It was not until the bird's third year that a persistent female dove resisted his attempts to drive her away and they mated. Although they bred successfully for many years, the male frequently left his mate in the breeding season to display before pigeons. Räber's (1948) account of attachment of a domestic turkey to a man or human dummy clearly indicates the potential relevance of particular releasing stimuli. A man was the object of sexual advances and so was any object on the ground, e.g. a boot, which approached the size of a hen. Anything with flapping or trailing features, e.g. a woman in a skirt or a man with a brief-case, was attacked. Hormonal features were probably relevant, since these responses did not occur during the moult. A more complicated case is reported by Kear (1960) of a female Hawfinch (*Coccothraustes coccothraustes*) which had been hand-reared by other workers and had had a courtship, though not a successful mating, with a sibling. During its third year, when kept in a room with cages of other birds, the bird, which originally showed fear of the experimenter, began to display feebly towards her. This developed progressively to the extent that, by the spring of the sixth year, other people were threatened and incipient nesting procedures were addressed to Kear.

However, what appears to be a fairly straightforward result of propinquity and imprinting is reported by Schutz (1965b, 1966). Over several years, studies with Mallard ducklings have shown that Mallard males can be rendered homosexual by rearing them in small flocks of five to ten for 75 days or more. When liberated on to the lake at Seewiesen, and despite the presence of large numbers of female Mallards, they form homosexual pairs in which neither appears to be ready to accept the passive role of the female, but attempts to maintain the role of the male. Many unsuccessful attempts at copulation thus occur, without apparent damage to the relationship, which lasts for many years and possibly (subject to further study) for the remainder of the bird's life. Females reared under similar conditions do not become homosexual, possibly since in this species the male differs in appearance from the female, which also appears to have a stronger and more prescriptive innate releasing mechanism for sexual responses.

EARLY IMPRINTING AND LATER SEXUAL ATTACHMENTS

A general facilitating effect in mating behaviour appears to derive from early social experience; but Wood-Gush (1958), in comparing the responses of Brown Leghorn cocks reared socially and in isolation for six months with sexually experienced pullets, found no very marked differences. Brief periods of social living with hens, however, improved the mating activity of any unresponsive cocks. As Kruijt (1962, 1964) found with longer periods of isolation, deprived cocks react very aggressively towards the females and, in the view of Wood-Gush, some time is necessary for alignment of the sexual and aggressive motivation. A consistent finding is reported by Siegel and Siegel (1964) with domestic cockerels (unstated strain), groups of which were reared in sex-intermingled flocks for 58, 70 and 84 days. Thereafter they were transferred to all-male groups or to individual cages. No visual or auditory isolation was involved, but contact was prevented in the individual cages. Mating behaviour with females was tested at 217 to 231 days in eight sessions, each of 10 minutes, and all in the afternoon, with no cock taking more than one test per day. Once again, the socially housed birds mounted and trod more readily; but those transferred at 58 days gave the most significant results, followed by those transferred at 70 days. Homosexual behaviour was common in all-male groups. Schein *et al.* (1962) have shown that White Leghorn chicks reared with Turkey poults showed a preference for their rearing partners when adult. They introduce the concept of 'taxonomic proximity' to explain why attachments to human attendants are sometimes relinquished when conspecific females are available.

A similar result is reported by Warriner *et al.* (1963) with White King and Black King pigeons. These were used because, while similar in size and breeding habits, they differ clearly in colour. Breeding cages were carefully covered so that the young birds saw only their parents. In testing sessions, 16 mature birds were in the cage during periods of observation, permitting a range of choice to the 32 male birds, 26 of which mated with birds of the same colour as their parents. This is very significant statistically. Only 14 of 32 females mated with a bird of the same colour as the parents, which is not significant. The authors suggest that mating in these pigeons is dominated by the male; but differences between the sexes will be noticed again.

Guiton (1962) has reported further definite evidence of the influence of early imprinting. Persistent sexual fixations on human beings by Brown Leghorn cocks, deriving from early association, were apparent a year later but, as not infrequently observed, hens were preferred if available. In other experiments, Guiton (1961) used three groups. All the individuals of one group were imprinted from two to five days on a box equipped with a speaker. Those in the second group were imprinted on a box of different shape, also sounding, in subgroups of five. Members of the third group received no training but each individual was exposed to one of the models for habituation, just before it was six weeks old. The trained birds tended to follow the models, with some decline in response as is usual in this type of experiment, until they were between 8 and 12 weeks of age, with a more intense response and better discrimination of models from the individually trained birds. It was also noted that the imprinted birds, especially at about eight weeks of age, acted aggressively towards their models and some of them waltzed. These responses were more frequent in the individually housed birds than those exposed to the model in groups; but no comparable responses were observed in the 'no training', i.e. non-imprinted, group.

In a later experiment, Guiton (1966) used two groups of male Brown Leghorn chicks. Group 1 was housed from hatching until day 20 in a communal brooder and from day 20 to day 47 in individual cages, visually isolated from one another. Group 2 went straight from the incubator to isolation cages where they remained till day 47. Whenever they were fed or watered or later injected, the experimenter wore a yellow rubber glove. On day 47 all birds were transferred to a single large pen with 10 pullets and left there for three days, when each male was returned to its individual cage. Meanwhile, on days 4, 25 and 46 all birds had been injected with testosterone oenanthate. Discrimination tests were held on days 47 and 51, i.e. just before and after the social experience with the pullets. The chicks, standing in the middle of the runway, had a choice between a stuffed pullet in crouching position and a stuffed yellow glove. In the first series of tests, on day 47, the isolates (group 2) copulated significantly less with the pullet but significantly more with the glove, which they had often seen. Only one member of group 1 attempted to copulate with or waltzed to the glove. In a second series of tests, on day 51, after the three days in the mixed-sex group, the members of group 2 were still copulating significantly more often with the glove, but their copulation with the model pullet had so improved that the differences between the groups was no longer significant. Guiton is of the opinion that bodily contact between chicks is important for the development of the copulatory response and mentions the possibility, raised by Fisher and Hale (1957), that whereas copulatory behaviour requires a background of social experience for normal development, the pattern of the waltz may be innate.

A variation of the above experimental design was introduced by Bambridge (1962), who arranged his experiments in three phases. In the first phase, (New Hampshire × Barred Rock) chicks were exposed either to a blue or a yellow moving object within the first two days when, it was held, the critical or optimal period for imprinting is operative. The same procedure was repeated with other chicks when the optimal period was thought to have passed. In a third phase, Barred Rock chicks were exposed to one of the objects under identical conditions but during a period which overlapped that used in phases 1 and 2. Birds in phases 1 and 3 were described as having contact with the model during following, but those in phase 2 hardly followed at all. From the fifth day of life the birds had injections of 0·5 mg testosterone propionate in 0·1 ml sesame oil. Later, on days 19 and 20, discrimination tests were held involving a choice between the blue and yellow objects, one of which had been experienced earlier. Birds trained wholly within the critical period trod the model significantly more than the other groups, which suggests that the more effective imprinting in respect of following, the more definite are the sexual responses when accelerated in this artificial way.

In a related study, Salzen (1966) used three experimental conditions with domestic chicks. In experiment 1 the chicks were isolated and the experimental birds were treated with testosterone oenanthate. In experiment 2 the experimental chicks were treated with the hormone, but both they and their controls had visual experience of a chick in a neighbouring compartment. In experiment 3 socially reared and isolated birds, both groups treated with hormone, and their controls had two minutes experience on alternate days of a hand placed in the cage. From day 7 to day 25 all chicks were tested at various times for their responses to a hand, a dead chick and a live chick of their own kind. The criteria in observation were fear, exploratory behaviour, sexual behaviour, indifference and aggression. Salzen, in this and other studies (1962), has emphasised the role of fear. When fear has been reduced by familiarity or by imprinting before fear has developed, approach of any kind to an object is easier. This thesis was to a large extent upheld in the present study. Fear of the prone hand was least in experiment 3, and fear of the live and of the dead chick was least in experiment 2. Where familiarity existed and fear was least, hormone-treated birds revealed the most sexual and aggressive behaviour. Their controls showed exploration and aggression. When fear was low, the occurrence of sexual or aggressive behaviour seemed to depend on the nature of the stimulus and the hormone level. As suggested herein several times, the formation of any kind of attachment is rarely simple.

Some further indications of the nature of sexual attachments emerge from the extensive studies of Schutz (1963–65), who takes the view that the following response and sexual attachment should be regarded as separate processes. One difficulty is, of course, that further painstaking studies of many species and variety of stimuli may reveal further significant differences in timing, but the evidence from Schutz's own studies with Mallards suggests that following and sexual attachment are separated in time. One-third of the birds kept from three to nine weeks with an imprinting object became sexually imprinted on the object, and, in another experiment, 7 out of 19 drakes first exposed to an imprinting partner at the age of slightly more than five days were found to be sexually imprinted. Whatever refinements in timing may appear from further study, exposure for the first 50 days to a sibling or foster mother of another species produces definite sexual attachments. Of 34 Mallard drakes exposed to a heterospecific partner (foster mother or sibling), 22 or 64% attempted to pair with a member of the species with which they had been reared, and in circumstances permitting a wide choice. In this type of attachment, the foster mother was found to be the more satisfactory object, possibly because the size of a bird of the same age would change appreciably during the period of exposure. Schutz (see 1965a) also found clear evidence of what he calls the 'balance principle', the balance between the pre-scriptive influence of innate factors and the acquired. While male Mallards can be sexually imprinted on a variety of rearing partners, female Mallards tend to mate with their own species, regardless of the circumstances. Mallards are a sexually dimorphic species, the male being a more striking and colour-ful bird than the more uniformly coloured female. In the case of the female, to use Schutz's image, the balance beam is longer on the innate side. In the Chilean Teal (*Anas flavirostris*), where the sexes are alike in appearance, the females will mate with species upon which they have been imprinted.

Sexual imprinting appears to be fairly widespread among other waterfowl and has been observed among Sheld-ducks, the Wood and Muscovy ducks and the Red-crested Pochards, but despite the very useful lead which Schutz has given, the relationship between early imprinting, as indicated by the exclusive following of a particular object or species and later sexual attachment, requires further investigation. The solution might be a little clearer if more were known of:

(i) the intrinsic attraction of particular stimuli and combinations of stimuli, the relative duration of their attraction and, in addition, the properties of arousal of different stimulus combinations for various forms of behaviour;

(ii) the relative difficulty of learning and retaining impressions of different conformations of objects;

(iii) the influence of familiarity, which may be easier to attain with some objects, on fear and readiness to learn new patterns of stimulation;

(iv) the perceptual qualities of objects, if any, which are erotically stimulating;

(v) the degree of continuity between early, partial aspects of patterns of sexual behaviour and the normal adult pattern.

Early imprinting at least should increase the probability of a later sexual attachment to the same type of object because of prior familiarity and the possibility of proximity when some phases of the sexual process begin to develop.

6. Activities Resembling Imprinting in Mammals

As already emphasised in Chapter 1, phenomena analogous to and not necessarily identical with imprinting in birds occur in a number of species. The pressure of survival may well favour by selection the evolution of the ability of the young of many species to form a discriminative response very rapidly, and the fact that this occurs in such diverse species as insects, birds and mammals is not itself an argument for evolutionary continuity of the structures mediating the discrimination.

Stable preferences for particular types of objects may develop in several ways, by slow habituation, by rewarded or reinforced learning and by imprinting, the chief characteristic of which is the achievement of an effective discrimination and attachment after a brief exposure. Since, as already shown, attachment has reinforcing value and the unreinforced approaches of an imprinting process can be improved by rewards of food, it is difficult, especially with mammals, where approach to the mother is directly associated with nutritive rewards, to decide where the imprinting-like process ends and rewarded learning begins.

Newly born lambs, goats, foals and the calves of camels, moose and domestic cows will approach, on becoming mobile, the nearest large object in the vicinity. This is normally the mother and there may be, because of natural selection, some insurance against interference of this first important association, since the mother usually withdraws from the herd before the birth. Smith (1965), Smith *et al.* (1966) were able to study in some detail the lambing of domestic breeds of sheep, Clun Forest, Mule (Hexham Leicester ram × Swaledale ewe) and

Half-Breed (Border Leicester ram × Cheviot ewe). For some time before the rupture of the amnion, the ewe was observed to be grazing apart from the flock, and with the rupture of this sac she began to sniff the grass on which the amniotic fluid had fallen. It proved very difficult to move the ewe away from this area. Even if, for experimental purposes, she was gently driven away, she usually contrived to return and it was here, after labour, the lamb was born. Sometimes ewes having their first lamb appeared bewildered; but the first sounds of struggling by the wet lamb, and particularly its first weak bleating, precipitated the process of nuzzling and licking of the neonate. This was accompanied by a low-pitched and rumbling bleat from the ewe, so that the lamb did receive tactile, auditory and visual stimulation, and had ample opportunity to learn the vocal characteristics of the mother. The ewe, by licking the amniotic fluid from the grass, was probably being put in a state of readiness for the next important stage, the nuzzling and licking of the lamb, and in fact the process analogous to olfactory imprinting of the ewe upon the lamb could be regarded as beginning when the ewe begins to sniff the amniotic fluids on the grass. The probability of the ewe finding the lamb is also enhanced by this process – see plates III a and III b.

In the lamb's approach to the teat, there is evidence of an instinctive pattern. The relevant activating stimulus is anything under which the lamb can thrust its head. The lower rail of a fence, the bulge of trousers overlapping the top of the observer's knee-boots, several models with overhanging ledges about the height of the lamb's shoulder, a folded overcoat hanging over a trestle, the front shoulder and the neck of the ewe were all approached by the lamb. The head was repeatedly thrust underneath, with the butting movements and peculiar shaking of the tail which is typical of suckling behaviour in lambs. The finding of the teat, and an effective orientation to it, was in many cases a relatively slow process extending in some cases over an hour and probably aided by smell. In a series of experiments in which lambs were born on to a disposable polythene sheet and the ewe moved immediately to a clean pen in a distant barn, it was possible to study the process by which the ewe comes to discriminate and become attached to the lamb. By returning lambs to the ewes at different intervals, Smith *et al.* (1966) were able to conclude, for the breeds studied, that the ewe would accept any lamb, not necessarily her own, up to at least eight hours after giving birth; within that period, any lamb which was presented to her and licked for between 20 and 30 minutes was fully accepted and allowed to suckle. No more than two lambs were presented to any one ewe. One at least was not her own. In all, 37 lambs were returned to 21 ewes with only one case of immediate refusal, which was accepted some 35 minutes later.

By recording the bleating of individual lambs, Smith (1965) was able to establish that ewes which had been tending their lambs for four or five days would reveal agitated searching and bleating at the absence of one or both of their lambs and were capable of finding the source of the recorded bleats when the tape-recorder was hidden around several corners of barns and in competition with the many noises of the flock. Grabowski (1941) has reported evidence of a hand-fed lamb which came to recognise the voice of its human 'nurse' and was capable of distinguishing his voice and person from among a group of ten soldiers; but this discrimination could have reflected some rewarded learning.

The power of the ewe to discriminate her own lambs is usually mediated by olfactory cues. Young lambs will suckle greedily from any ewe; but strangers, after a quick sniff, are almost invariably butted away by the ewe, and the survival of the lamb is probably best ensured by having one ewe dedicated to its nutrition. Klopfer *et al.* (1964) obtained rather more dramatic results with Toggenburg goats. One group of 14 does ('immediate separation group') were deprived of their kids as soon as they were born and had no opportunity to lick them. A second group of does were allowed 5 minutes of nuzzling or licking of the newborn kid, which occasionally was interrupted by the birth of another and might range up to 10 minutes but was rarely more than 6 minutes. Kids were returned after 1, 2 or 3 hours and the experimenters took 10 minutes in which to judge acceptance or rejection. In the 'immediate separation group', 12 out of 14 rejected their kids. Of the 'prior contact group' (only 5 minutes contact), 2 out of 14 rejected, which is a very significant statistical result. The fact of more than one kid and the duration of separation made no discernible difference. Five minutes was crucial and blind-folding had no effect. Olfactory cues appear to be essential. Such a finding suggests a possible explanation of an interesting observation by Blauvelt (1955). As soon as the newborn kid becomes mobile, the doe, in normal circumstances, maintains a 'safe' area around it. Intruders are butted away and after the butting the mother circles the kid, in effect ensuring free-dom from interruption and favourable conditions for the attachment of mother and young.

In a species which is mobile, rapid and effective attach-ments have obvious survival value and would tend to arise and be maintained by selective pressure. But there is another aspect of selection. Kids whose 'safe' territory has not been main-tained, because of accident or experimental design, do not develop a normal social life. It is soon apparent that they lack confidence and poise in social relationships with other kids. Invitations to play are received with aggressive butting and, before long, communication is so bad that other kids react to it as an inanimate object. At six months the kid is not only backward socially, but tends to be below normal weight. Liddell (1960) found that kids separated from the mother for periods of from 30 minutes to 2 hours, soon after birth, with-stood the strain of conditioning techniques much worse than controls. Within the first year of life, 19 out of 22 separated kids had died, compared with 2 out of 22 controls. One sur-viving female, which had suffered separation soon after birth, proved to be a most inefficient mother to a male kid which died at the age of 15 months. He, in marked con-trast with a matched control male born to an undeprived mother, was found to be indifferent to the females of the flock, and at *post-mortem* his testes were found to have atrophied.

The relevance of olfactory cues in discrimination and at-tachment has been further illustrated by Klopfer and Gamble

(1966). They again confirmed that rejection of the kid was uncommon if the doe was allowed to nuzzle and lick the kid five minutes after birth. They had only 2 rejections out of 17 does, and these two had never before reared young. Of the 14 deprived of their young immediately at birth, 13 later rejected. In a further experiment, does were treated with a spray of a cocaine solution, inserted into the nostril before the birth. This did not lead to the rejection of their own young by any of the six does so treated, but it seriously interfered with the discrimination between their own and other kids, which would normally be rejected. In another experiment, the olfactory impairment was induced after the does had licked the kids. The spray was applied in the nostrils before the acceptance tests and four out of seven does rejected their own young, which they had previously licked. It would appear that inability to obtain an impression, which matched the original odours, contributed to the rejection. It was found, too, that whatever the reaction obtained at the tests, it persisted when the effects of the cocaine had worn off. This could be due in part to hesitancy on the part of lambs which had been rejected.

Despite the readiness with which the attachment appears to take place in goats, it can be offset by slow habituation. Hersher *et al.* (1963) resorted to what in effect is an old shepherd's trick, of securing the head of the ewe to prevent butting and enable the young to suckle. They cross-fostered kids on to ewes and lambs to does, between 2 and 12 hours after parturition. All of the adoptions were established by an average of 10 days and there were few differences between foster mothers and controls rearing their own young. There was a positive correlation between the length of time necessary for full acceptance and the strength of the mother's reaction to separation, and generally the cross-species foster mothers reacted more vigorously to separation.

The possibility of the lamb contributing to the attachment has been indicated by Alexander and Williams (1966) in studies of fine-wool Merino sheep. By fitting covers over the teats, they established that the proportion of time spent in teat-seeking declines from about 30% during the first 3 hours of life to less than 5% at 12 hours after birth. This initial peak may not be solely due to hunger, because teat-seeking activity was not completely suppressed by giving the lambs milk in the first hours of life, and in any event hunger could be expected to increase with the passing hours, whereas teat-seeking decreases. The same authors also indicated with older lambs, that the amount of grooming by the ewe, or artificial grooming by the experimenter, was positively related to the amount of teat-seeking and gain in weight.

Another series of observations suggesting a phenomenon analogous to imprinting are those of Altmann (1958) on the Moose *Alces alces*. The moose calf does not become effectively mobile until about the fourth day after birth, when its marked following or 'heeling' of the moose cow is evident and may be addressed to a variety of moving animals, including a man on horseback, if the calf becomes separated from its mother. At about the age of 20 days, when the range of activity has widened, it is evident that the cow is maintaining a territory around the calf by driving other moose away and the calf back into the 'safe radius', when it has strayed. Shipley (1963) has also provided evidence of a process resembling imprinting in guinea pigs (*Cavia cutteri*). In several experiments it was found that animals exposed to a rotating white octagonal block would later approach it, and that this ability could be retained for several weeks with only slight opportunities for revision. It was also possible to elicit quite strong responses from animals which had been exposed to the mother for five days, then isolated and exposed to the block at day 7 and day 9. Andrew (1964), reporting Shipley's work, has instanced seven males which were isolated from the mother five days after birth and on the second and fourth days after separation were exposed to the white moving block for five minutes. At ages ranging from 47 to 103 days, they were injected with testosterone oenanthate after being exposed again to the moving block for five minutes. Two days later, these experimental animals were observed to be mounting the block significantly more than controls. The broad similarity with Andrew's (1964) results with injected chickens, which prematurely mounted the imprinting object, is apparent, but in this case no pelvic thrusts or ejaculation were observed.

McBride (1963) has drawn attention to the remarkable rapidity with which 'teat order' is established in pigs, very often before the last piglet is born. If the litter is taken away and mixed up, they are all back on their correct teat within two minutes. A variety of cues such as sight and smell may help, but McBride thinks that the pattern in the 'lie' of the hair on the belly of the sow is helpful. The relevant considera- tion is that the piglets appear able to recognise and go to their particular teat with very little opportunity for learning. This might be due to a direct cue or to a rapidly formed 'imprint' or impression of the position of the teat. Ewer (1960) has observed a similar 'teat constancy' which kittens establish during the first four days of life. Each kitten in this period establishes ownership of one teat and rarely feeds from another. This constancy is well maintained until the litter begin to range beyond the nest, when there is some reduction. Ewer does not accept the suggestion that the cue is that each nipple has a characteristic odour, because the mother freq- uently licks the teats. Observation points to topographical cues, but confirmation is needed. It is conceivable that the pressure of selection could favour constancy. Constancy would prob- ably favour greater efficiency in feeding and survival. Nipples function better if regularly exercised, and in natural circum- stances the litter would tend to settle down more quickly and leave the mother more time for hunting.

Some evidence of induced attachment by dogs to a white circle lit by intermittent light is offered by Marr (1964). Nine litters of pure-bred dogs, comprising 8 Miniature Poodles, 10 English Cockers, 7 German Shepherds and 5 Shetland Sheep- dogs were divided into three major groups. At three weeks of age, the experimental group were exposed to the white disc for three trials per day under intermittent illumination, and at the same time they were rubbed and rocked. Control animals were either not exposed to the disc or exposed without any stimulation. In tests at the age of four weeks, those which had received the varying stimulation were found to be much more attached to the disc than the other two groups, which did not differ between themselves. Igel and Calvin (1960), who worked with 16 mongrel puppies, found that of the four groups of puppies reared on wire- or cloth-covered models of female dogs, one of each providing milk, a marked liking for the contact of the cloth was established, but unlike the preference reported of chimpanzees for texture, the dogs tended to spend more time near the lactating mother.

Quite the reverse is reported by Harlow and Zimmerman (1959) of the extensive studies carried out at the University of Wisconsin on the affectional responses of infant (usually Rhesus) monkeys. Crude wire-frame 'mothers' and the same frames covered with soft cloth were used. Both types could be provided with nipples giving milk, if necessary. Studies have commenced when the animals were within 6 to 12 hours from birth. The monkeys involved usually gain 25% more weight than those in the care of normal mothers. There can be no doubt of very genuine attachment to the cloth mother and this was basically a matter of contact. Removal of the cloth was always associated with deep emotional distress. Those feeding in the frames preferred the cloth mother. At times of anxiety the young ape fled to the cloth mother and, with the cloth mother present, the animals could face new and frightening situations without undue emotion. The wire mother did not afford this support. There was evidence, too, that the affection for the cloth mother was retained. Apes which had lived with the surrogate mothers for 165 to 170 days and were separated and tested for the following 9 days and then at intervals of 30 days during the following year, still revealed an attraction for the cloth mother, as did those in another experiment with animals which had been separated for 15 months. It would be instructive, from the point of view of those interested in imprinting, to determine whether or not the young apes, who seem to be so much influenced by tactile impressions, could discriminate between different textures after brief contact – see Plate V.

Several features noted of imprinting in birds are apparent

in the foregoing studies of mammals. There is the rapid acquisition of discrimination and enduring attachment which takes place most readily during early life. The nature of this attachment is clearly associated with later development and this theme will be examined in the next chapter.

7. Wider Implications for the Study of Children

Yet again it is emphasised that wherever in studies of children some processes may resemble imprinting, the apparent similarity should not be regarded as satisfactory evidence of evolutionary continuity. The life span of human beings is normally much longer than that of other animals, and the range of experience and learning is generally greater. Moreover, attachments and fixations in human groups occur in a different context. But objective studies have indicated some interesting stages.

Schaffer and Emerson (1964) made a very careful study of the reactions of 60 infants (31 male) in a variety of circumstances, such as being left alone in a room, alone in the pram outside the house or shops, and on being set down after being held. They found that specific attachments had usually been achieved by about the age of nine months, subject of course to the effects of illness and disturbances in family organisation. Their graph of specific attachment actually reaches its peak at 41 to 44 weeks, and the object in 93% of cases was the mother; but other persons, father, aunt or grandmother, might be the principal object of attachment if they spent more time near the child. The attachment falls slightly as the child becomes more mobile by crawling and walking. In general, the infant with a strong attachment to a principal object was more likely to have the greater range of minor attachments to other objects in the environment, but to be more afraid of complete strangers at the first meeting.

This general order of development is not inconsistent with

91

other studies of early social reactions. Hetzer and Tudor-Hart (1927), for example, found that babies at two months reacted indiscriminately to hand-clapping, a kindly voice, an angry voice, a singing voice and a variety of other sounds. Bühler and Hetzer (1928) reported that their infant subjects ranged in age from five to seven months before they appeared to differentiate between scowling and smiling faces. Kaila (1932), working with 71 infants of the same national and cultural background from a single institution, came to the conclusion that between the age of three and six months, the baby's smile to a smiling human face is not interpretative or imitative, but a response to a configuration or gestalt. This gestalt or pattern must include certain basic characteristics such as two eyes, a nose and a smooth forehead, and motion in the rest of the face which could take the form of smiling or nodding of the head. If the observer covered his eyes or turned the face in profile, smiling ceased. Spitz (1946a) came to a similar conclusion from a study of 251 children (112 female) of White, Coloured and North American Indian race, drawn from private homes delivery clinics and nurseries. The necessary elements of the configuration were a forehead, two eyes, a nose and some movement in the mouth–nose region. These elements could be embodied in a scowling human face, and all but one of the 142 infants tested between the third and sixth month smiled. Crude models such as a Hallowe'en mask or a scarecrow face, if tapped from behind to give movement in the mouth–nose area, gave similar results. After the age of six months, the efficacy of the models tended to decline and there was evidence that instead of smiling at any face embodying the basic elements for the smiling response, the infant began to smile only to one or a few faces which he or she had come to know. Throughout this extensive study, there was evidence that children living in institutions, as a class, tended to be backward while those from a kindly home environment tended to be advanced in development.

A similar picture arises from the study of Ahrens (1954), who obtained smiling responses in the early months to simple patterns of black dots on a white background, roughly resembling a human face. As the age approached six months, however, more differentiation became necessary, such as eyes, eyebrows and mouth; after six months, models evoked fewer smiles until only a human face and one or two particular and familiar human faces could evoke a smile. Later, and as other studies by Ambrose (1960) have shown, smiling responses may be extended to others; but as the child grows older, factors of learning and interpretation enter to an increasing extent. Gray (1958) puts the 'critical period' for the evocation of smiles by configurations at six weeks to six months, but Spitz in his extensive study recorded the earliest smiles at 20 days. It is interesting and indicative of Charles Darwin's interest in behaviour that he made close observations (1877) on two children and recorded the first definite smiles at 45 to 46 days, a result which many later studies have confirmed.

Salzen (1963b) distinguishes between the 'gastric' smile, i.e. to gastric stimuli, and smiling to a visual stimulus which he first recorded at about seven to eight weeks. Not unlike Ahrens, he found that very simple stimuli, such as a contrast in brightness, typified by a flashing torch or a card with sectors painted on it, were effective. The baby girl would stop feeding and smile at these stimuli. By the eleventh week, sound stimuli were found to be of assistance and, as other workers have found, more complex stimuli were necessary as the weeks went by. It is of interest that the first social response of a human baby and the domestic chick and duckling, and the wild partridge and pheasant can be evoked by the same stimulus. It may be that anything, however vague, which is capable of capturing attention, will elicit some positive response, approach in the case of precocial birds and smiling in the case of infants. Further acquaintance brings increasing knowledge of details and discrimination. It is only by awareness of something other than oneself that knowledge of oneself and a basis of orientation can be acquired. Banham (1950) has, in fact, constructed a whole theory of the development of the affectional life on a similar concept of 'outgoing'.

THE CONSEQUENCES OF DEPRIVATION

The intellectual retardation of children living in institutions has frequently been noted and will be treated later. Some idea of the possible consequences of sensory deprivation may derive from an account of some extreme instances with adults, who can be more explicit about their experiences than infants and young children.

Scott *et al.* (1959) deprived 29 male subjects aged from 19 to 30 years (average 22 years) of a considerable amount of sensory input by requiring them to reside, apart from meals and toilet functions, in a partially sound-proof cubicle into which diffuse scrambled noise was relayed. Lying on a soft, comfortable bed, they wore muffs on the hands and glasses which permitted only blurred vision. In effect, the subjects had no precise tactile, auditory or visual experience for three to four days. Although the subjects were well paid, only 18 stayed long enough to complete the first part of the test programme because, while none found the experience pleasant, some found it particularly disturbing. Several reported difficulty in controlling their thoughts and excessive enthusiasm when minor tasks and calculations were completed. Hallucinations were also reported. Tests including copying, detection of anomalies, and established intelligence tests, given during the period of isolation, gave significant differences which were consistently in favour of the controls. The experimental group were also more suggestible and likely to accept uncritically propaganda-type statements. A similar experiment by Doane *et al.* (1959), with the exception that some of the subjects wore opaque masks until one hour before the crucial tests, when a change to translucent masks was made, reported similar results. Compared with results of tests before isolation and those of control subjects, the most prominent effects were disturbances of size-constancy (knowledge of the size of objects despite their distance from the observer), colour adaptation, and after-effects of prolonged fixation. Again, subjects reported hallucinations and recordings of wave activity in the cortex by the electro-encephalograph revealed significant changes.

Further consistent reports on 17 men, some of whom remained in an 'iron-lung'-type respirator for periods up to 36 hours, were provided by Wexler *et al.* (1958). The interesting fact was that several asked to be released, because of genuine anxiety and panic. While in the respirator most subjects reported inability to concentrate. Performance at simple arithmetical problems and judgements of time were poor. Illusions and hallucinations were common. Lilly (1956) was able to obtain comparable results by allowing his subjects to float in a tank of warm water, but emphasised in addition the shock to the ego induced by the realisation of being severed from normal contact with the environment and the improved ability of subjects to withstand the stress if they knew that the isolation had a definite terminus.

Now, these are only a few of several studies which might be cited, indicating how rapid and severe are the effects of experimentally contrived, sensory deprivation. The interesting fact is that these findings can be related to a large number of historical events. Alain Bombard (1963), medical practitioner and researcher in the physiology of survival, who crossed the Atlantic in a small rubber raft, explains how he was provoked into taking an interest in psychological problems of survival. Some 40 sailors, taken from a vessel which had been wrecked on the coast nearby were brought into the hospital where he was on duty. He went immediately down to the casualty ward expecting little more than abrasions, fractures, shock and exposure. He found the great majority unconscious and, despite the best efforts of the staff, they could not be revived. They had only had one night of exposure. Bombard feels that the blow to inertia and morale by the loss of 'my' ship, which had been their home, plus the inevitable fear, had taken toll of their resistance to combat the additional strains of exposure. He himself in his Atlantic crossing suffered bouts of depression and undue elation, loss of confidence in his power to navigate and just plain inefficiency. These aberrations appear in the reports of most lone navigators, from Slocum (repr. 1963) to Chichester (1967). To Slocum, writhing one night in his bunk on the *Spray* with a digestive upset, appeared the pilot of

Columbus's vessel, the *Pinta*, who informed him that he need not worry about the navigation. On the next morning, the *Spray* was 80 miles further ahead, and on course. Slocum did not try to explain the hallucination. He merely recorded it. Admiral Byrd (1958), alone for several months in the Antarctic, had very few hallucinations, but noted a marked falling off in his capacity to work and confidence in his own judgement, although some aggravation from slow carbon monoxide poisoning was very probable. Gibson (1953) and Tiira (1954) recorded, from actual experience, the peculiar lethargy preceding death which overcame survivors in small craft and regressions of behaviour which are possible in some personalities under stress. However, a considerable restoration of faith in human nature is to be gained from the account by Gaddis (1957) of the remarkable performance of Robert Stroud (*The Birdman of Alcatraz*), who survived with personality, integrity and efficiency intact. When the book was finished in 1955, Stroud was 65 and had endured nearly 40 years of solitary confinement. Interesting and admirable though less epic accounts, which stress the importance of personality in combating isolation, are those of Burney (1961) and Ritter (1954).

A similar picture emerges from reports by Hinkle and Wolff (1956), Schein (1956) and Lifton (1956). Solitary confinement, physical discomfort and the deliberate 'planting' of false information can do much to shake a prisoner's faith in his own judgement and even the continuity of his own experience. Great concentration is necessary to withstand months of cross-questioning and to rebut cleverly contrived and impossible accusations, based upon slight twists of one's own evidence. The natural tendency, from sheer exhaustion, is to confess anything to put an end to the strain. Yet some survive; but of those prisoners who have renounced allegiance to their native land, the majority are persons of low education and social attainment in their own country and lacking in a firm basis of emotional allegiance.

STUDIES OF SENSORY AND MATERNAL DEPRIVATION IN ANIMALS

A vast literature is available and indication of more than a few studies and trends is impossible here, but the same general thesis emerges. Animals incurring sensory and maternal deprivation are less efficient and less resistant to stress. Clark *et al.* (1951) found that inbred Scotch Terriers, reared in isolation apart from some association with human attendants, were more hesitant, inferior in simple test situations and below the weight of controls. Thompson and Heron (1954) reported similar results with their Scotch Terriers including the lower weight of the experimental group, and Melzack and Thompson (1956) found considerable social retardation among puppies reared in isolation. Nissen *et al.* (1951) have drawn attention to the repetitive movements of captive chimpanzees, in particular rocking and other repetitive movements. The pacing to and fro of captive animals might be an attempt to obtain more varied stimulation and, if this reduced boredom or stress, it could be self-reinforcing and thus prolonged. Similar observations, including head-shaking tics, are reported by Levy (1944) of a wide range of captive animals such as horses, bears, lions, tigers, wolves and jaguars. He also reported a heavy incidence of stereotyped movements among children in orphanages.

On the other hand, there is a large and growing body of evidence that animals which receive more stimulation in infancy are not only more active socially and more successful in problem solving, but also more resistant to stress. To cite only a few studies, Levine and Otis (1958) found that rats handled or 'gentled' before weaning were later found to have increased significantly in body weight and to have a higher survival rate than controls and those handled or gentled after weaning. Levine (1962) has also shown that rats stimulated in infancy survive better after severe stress. Even the administration of mild electric shocks from day 11 to day 20 was later found in adult rats by Denenberg and Smith (1963) to be associated with lower emotionality. Denenberg and Bell (1960) have shown too that light electric shocks, administered optimally between day 2 and day 9, enable mice when adult to

learn more readily to respond to stimuli which enable them
to avoid shocks. Meyers (1962) demonstrated that the simple
practice of carrying the brood box, containing the mother rat
and pups, some 40 ft to the end of the laboratory and back
was associated with increased exploratory activity, as compared with controls, at the age of 61 days. The best results
were obtained by those receiving this simple form of stimulation between the age of 6 and 10 days. Forgus (1955) found,
too, that male rats reared from day 25 to day 85 in cages containing a range of manipulative objects performed very significantly better, after a further seven days residence with controls in another cage, in learning to run a maze. The controls
had been able to see but not make contact with the objects.

Again, Ader *et al.* (1960) have shown that rats separated
from the mother at 15 days, i.e. before the time of normal
weaning, were later significantly more susceptible to gastric
ulcers in conflict situations than those weaned at the normal
time. In a later experiment, Ader and Friedmann (1965) injected different groups of rats with a suspension of Walker 256
carcinosarcoma. Those groups which were handled or gentled
during the pre-weaning period showed a significant retardation
in tumour development, relative to controls.

MATERNAL DEPRIVATION IN CHILDREN

In a most sensitive study entitled *The Rights of Infants*,
Margaret Ribble (1943) emphasises the uncertain hold which
an infant has upon life during the first few months. It is in this
early period that bodily contact with another person, gentle
rocking and low rhythmic sounds have a particularly reassuring and stabilising effect. Successful sucking responses often
depend upon a sympathetic approach and prior stimulation
of the tongue and palate. The touching dependence of Harlow's
baby apes upon contact with a cloth mother indicate just how
dependent is the early life upon the simple fact of reassuring
contact, which in Ribble's view does much, along with gentle
rocking and crooning, to stabilise breathing in the human
infant. As many studies cited in Chapter 7 have shown, clear
recognition of particular persons in the environment is not

achieved by the child until about half-way through the first year, and this development may be retarded if the infant has not achieved varied and adequate sensory stimulation, a condition which may not be met by the impersonal regimen of a large hospital. The basic needs seem clear: namely, a definite attachment to some one person, reinforced by warm contact and the many acts of care and solicitude, to serve as a basis of orientation for a varied range of stimulation. If this is not available, several phases of development are retarded, and in extreme cases a condition known as 'marasmus', a state of stupor with the implication of wasting, may occur. When, in the second half of the first year, behaviour becomes a little more explicit, additional observations are possible.

Spitz and Wolf (1945), in a study of 123 infants ranging in age from 6 to 12 months, reported in detail on 19 cases in whom they had noted prevalent weeping which later gave way to marked rigidity or withdrawal in response to social approaches, also insomnia, loss of weight and a gradual decline in the rate of development. Careful investigation showed, that, in all cases, the child had been separated from its mother somewhere between the sixth and the eighth month. They were impressed with the similarity between this syndrome, which they termed 'anaclitic depression', and that described by Abraham and Freud as the pathological mourning for the loss of the loved object. The infant cannot express his loss or resentment directly nor do anything constructive to offset the deprivation; but as he grows older, evidence of his chagrin can be expressed not only by withdrawal, as does the piqued child who refuses to play or participate in social activities, but also in sustained hostility.

The sense of attachment so necessary in early life becomes, with greater awareness of the social environment, a sense of solicitude, the conviction that someone cares about oneself. If the conviction is achieved, an important source of reassurance and orientation is available to help in meeting the feelings of doubt, anxiety and guilt, associated with growing up, until the maturing personality has acquired the width of orientation to ensure a measure of independence. If this conviction is not achieved, despite opportunities which may occur apart from parents, the probability of a satisfactory adjustment to society is lowered. The uneasy feeling of bewilderment or the sense of having been cheated can be associated with acts ranging from poor response to social demands, such as may be manifested in minor delinquencies, to active hostility, such as violence or failure at school, with the object of distressing the parent or guardian or just hitting out blindly against an intolerable situation. The reasons why one is resentful against parents or anything else would in many cases be unclear or unconscious to the child, but none the less powerful.

Bowlby (1951), in his monograph *Maternal Care and Mental Health*, gathered together a large amount of data ranging from deprivation in hospitals and institutions to wartime separation and brutality. His readers might gather the impression that the aftermath of maternal deprivation is inevitable and more serious than is now generally believed; but it should be remembered that studies in this field deal in probabilities. Failure to achieve a conviction of solicitude or a disturbance of the attachment of mother and child increased the *probability* of maladjustment. This leaves open the possibilities which are frequently noted, of exceptional cases which appear to have triumphed over every disability; but although available space permits the mention of only a few studies, there can be no doubt that maternal deprivation in early life enhances the likelihood of maladjustment.

Durfee and Wolf (1933) correlated the retardation of 118 infants in institutions with the amount of maternal care known to have been received. One noteworthy finding was that the most severe retardation was among those who had spent more than eight months of their first year in an institution. Spitz and Wolf (1945) reported arresting differences in development over the period 4 to 12 months for 61 children living in an institution, when compared with 103 children living with their mothers. Goldfarb (see 1943a to 1945) compared the mental development of children brought up until the age of three in an institution and then placed in foster homes with those who had gone directly from their mothers to a foster home in which they remained. In the majority of cases, the child left the mother within the first nine months of life. The sample most thoroughly studied consisted of 15 pairs, one member of which had lived in an institution, noted for the high standard of its physical hygiene, from approximately 6 months to 3·5 years of age. The matching member of the pair had never been in an institution. The foster homes were carefully matched. The children were between 10 and 14 years of age at the time the crucial tests were administered. Goldfarb claimed significant differences in favour of the 'all foster home' group in intelligence (Wechsler scale), social maturity (Vineland scale), standardised tests of arithmetic, power of concentration and confidence.

Bowlby *et al.* (1956) studied a group of 64 children (41 boys) who had been admitted to a T.B. sanatorium before the age of four years, between 1 January 1940 to November 1948. In 1950, when the ages ranged from 6 years 10 months to 13 years 7 months and the children having left the sanatorium were widely scattered in 58 different schools, comparisons were made with three other members of the same class and age, who were taught also by the same teacher. The mean I.Q. of the sanatorium children was three points lower than that of the controls, approaching but not quite attaining statistical significance. The 'sanatorium' group, however, were significantly more prone to daydreaming and poorer in concentration. They were much more indifferent to competition in school work, but more prone to become violent in play.

Another aspect of the same problem is illustrated by the study of adoptions. Humphrey and Ounsted (1963), from a study of 80 legal adoptions (53 boys) in Oxford, mention among their findings the striking fact of the greater number of children adopted before the age of six months who attain an I.Q. of 110 or better, when compared with later adoptions. They found a very close correspondence between the intelligence of the adopting parents and of the children, an observation also recorded by Skeels and Harms (1948) in the U.S.A. There are some interesting implications. Those adopted in the first six months of life have a much better chance of forming a strong emotional bond with the adopting parents; but it is quite possible that those people who are prepared to adopt very young children are more dedicated and possibly more efficient parents. In the present study, those children adopted after the age of six months were, as a class, significantly more apt to steal or destroy property.

It is generally known that a period in hospital is sometimes a trying experience for young children. It may represent a serious rupture in the slow process of learning by which a baby comes to feel at home or familiar in his family circle. Schaffer (1958) has in fact provided a study of 76 infants admitted to a children's hospital between the ages of 3 to 51 weeks, with a length of stay ranging from 4 to 49 days (mean, 15·4 days). In a careful study of the children on return-ing home, two syndromes or distinctive patterns were found. For those under seven months on return, the 'global' syn-drome was apparent. The child seemed preoccupied with the environment. A toy presented to him would be disregarded while he scanned the room, and the mothers and visitors had the awkward feeling that the child was looking through them. Digestive upset was apparent in 16 cases, and there were in-stances of the child waking and crying. The 'overdependent' syndrome was more commonly found among those returning after seven months of age. Excessive crying, fear of strangers and clinging to the mother were the main features, and these ranged over 1 to 81 days with a mean duration of 14·7 days. Schaffer makes the interesting suggestion, which resembles a view proposed by Werner (1940), that very young children tend to be more merged with their environment and less aware of themselves as independent objects or persons within it. The close scanning of the global syndrome could thus arise from the child seeking a new mergence. The older child is more aware of himself and of isolation, hence the clinging to the mother, the most familiar object in a temporarily strange en-vironment.

Another interesting study of hospitalisation is that of Prugh et al. (1953). Two groups, each of 100 children ranging in age from 2 to 12 years, were matched as closely as possible for age, sex and diagnosis of illness of which there was a wide range. The average length of stay in hospital for the control group was eight days, and for the experimental group, six days. The experimental group received daily visits from the parents, who co-operated with the staff. There could be no doubt from the results that the experimental group were less disturbed by the experience of hospital; but the age distribution is of interest in the present context. Children under three years old showed the highest incidence of severe reactions (50% in controls, 37% in experimental group). From 6 to 12 years the incidence was 30% and 7 %.

Turning to the problem of delinquency, the picture is very clear. A broken home or evidence of stress and anxiety in early years is associated with a greater probability (not the certainty) of delinquency. This is the consistent finding from studies by the Gluecks (1934), Menut (1943), Bowlby (1944), Stott (1950) and many others. Again, the League of Nations survey (1938) of 530 prostitutes showed a particularly high incidence of unsatisfactory home life.

8. Retrospect

Despite the limitations of space, it will be apparent that a considerable literature has derived from the early observations and insight of Whitman and Heinroth, and that throughout all developmental studies there is a growing realisation of the potential importance of early experience and attachments. Improved psychometric scaling of the effectiveness of stimuli will result in greater precision and should help to clarify such issues as the particular nature of imprinting as distinguished from associative learning. As the studies of Gibson, Walk *et al.* (1958–59) on the improved discrimination of rats for stimulus objects with which they had lived would suggest, the distinction between imprinting and other ways of acquiring responses might be a problem of different placings on a long continuum. In any event, the continuing study of the neurophysiology of all types of learning can only contribute positively to such a solution.

As Gottlieb's (1967) studies would suggest, the role of embryonic stimulation should amply repay further study. Smith and Templeton's (1966) finding that the genetic contribution to the young chick's response to visual stimuli, while positive, did not attain statistical significance suggests that the great range of individual differences between the responsiveness of different chicks might be due in part to factors operating during the embryonic stage or at, or soon after, hatching. There is no dearth of problems.

The study of animal behaviour provides ample illustration for the truism that everything in the natural struggle for existence means something or has an explanation. To take one example, Tinbergen *et al.* (1962) have shown that the Black-headed Gull (*Larus ridibundus*) removes the shells from the nest when the chicks have hatched. From careful experiments, there is good evidence that anything capable of attracting attention is removed from the nest. Broken shells, presenting a variation in colour and contour, would enhance the probability of carrion crows and herring gulls finding the nest and chicks. Survival is enhanced for the descendants of those gulls who keep a clean nest.

References

ABERCROMBIE, B. and JAMES, H. 1961. *Anim. Behav.*, **9**, 205–212.
ADER, R., BEELS, C. C. and TATUM, R. 1960. *J. comp. physiol. Psychol.*, **53**, 455–458.
ADER, R., TATUM, R. and BEELS, C. C. 1960. *J. comp. physiol. Psychol.*, **53**, 446–454.
ADER, R. and FRIEDMAN, S. B. 1965. *J. comp. physiol. Psychol.*, **59**, 361–364.
AGAR, W. E., DRUMMOND, F. H. and TIEGS, O. W. 1935, 1942, 1948, 1954. *J. exp. Biol.*
AHRENS, R. 1954. *Z. angew. Psychol.*, **2**, 402–454, 599–633.
ALEXANDER, G. and WILLIAMS, D. 1964. *Science*, **146**, 665–666.
ALEXANDER, G. and WILLIAMS, D. 1966. *Anim. Behav.*, **14**, 166–167.
ALLEY, R. and BOYD, H. 1950. *Ibis*, **92**, 46–51.
ALTMANN, M. 1952. *Behaviour*, **4**, 116–143.
ALTMANN, M. 1958. *Anim. Behav.*, **6**, 155–159.
AMBROSE, J. A. 1960. Unpubl. thesis Ph.D., Lond.
ANDERSON, B. and MCCANN, S. M. 1955. *Acta physiol. scand.*, **33**, 336–346.
ANDREW, R. J. 1963. *J. comp. physiol. Psychol.*, **56**, 933–940.
ANDREW, R. J. 1964. *Anim. Behav.*, **12**, 542–548.
ANDREW, R. J. 1966a. *Anim. Behav.*, **14**, 485–500.
ANDREW, R. J. 1966b. *Anim. Behav.*, **14**, 501–505.
ARISTOTLE. (trans.) 1910. *Historia Animalium*. Clarendon Press, Oxford.
BACON, H. R., WARREN, J. M. and SCHEIN, M. W. 1962. *Anim. Behav.*, **10**, 239–243.
BAER, D. M. and GRAY, R. H. 1960. *Percept. Mot. Skills*, **10**, 171–174.
BAERENDS, G. P. and BAERENDS-VAN ROON, J. M. 1950. *Behaviour*, Supp. 1, 1–242.
BAMBRIDGE, R. 1962. *Science*, **136**, 259–260.
BANHAM, K. M. 1950. *J. Genet. Psychol.*, **76**, 283–289.
BARON, A. and KISH, G. B. 1960. *J. comp. physiol. Psychol.*, **53**, 459–463.
BARON, A., KISH, G. B. and ANTONITIS, J. J. 1962. *J. genet. Psychol.* **100**, 355–360.
BATESON, P. P. G. 1964a. *Nature*, **202**, 421–422.

BATESON, P. P. G. 1964b. *J. comp. physiol. Psychol.*, **57**, 100–103.

BATESON, P. P. G. 1964c. *J. comp. physiol. Psychol.*, **58**, 407–411.

BATESON, P. P. G. 1964d. *Anim. Behav.*, **12**, 479–489.

BATESON, P. P. G. 1964e. *Anim. Behav.*, **12**, 490–492.

BATESON, P. P. G. 1966. *Biol. Rev.*, **41**, 177–220.

BLAUVELT, H. 1955. In *Group Processes* (Schaffner, ed.), pp. 94–144. Josiah Macey Foundation, New York.

BOMBARD, A. 1963. *The Bombard Story* (translation). André Deutsch, London.

BOWLBY, J. 1944. *Int. J. Psycho-Analysis*, **25**, 107–128.

BOWLBY, J. 1951. *Maternal Care and Mental Health*. W.H.O., Geneva.

BOWLBY, J., AINSWORTH, M. B., BOSTON, M. and ROSENBLUTH, D. 1956. *Br. J. med. Psychol.*, **29**, 211–223.

BOYD, H. and FABRICIUS, E. 1965. *Behaviour*, **25** 1–15.

BROOM, D. M. 1966. *Anim. Behav.*, **14**, 586–587.

BROWN, L. T. 1964. *Anim. Behav.*, **12**, 353–361.

BRÜCKNER, G. H. 1933. *Z. Psychol.*, **128**, 1–120.

BÜHLER, C. and HETZER, H. 1928. *Z. Psychol.*, **107**, 50–61.

BURNEY, C. 1961. *Solitary Confinement*. Macmillan, London.

BYRD, R. E. 1958. *Alone*. Spearman, London.

CAMPBELL, B. A. and PICKLEMAN, J. R. 1961. *J. comp. physiol. Psychol.*, **54**, 592–596.

CARBAUGH, B. T., SCHEIN, M. W. and HALE, E. B. 1962. *Anim. Behav.*, **10**, 233–234.

CARR, A. and HIRTH, H. 1961. *Anim. Behav.*, **9**, 68–70.

CHICHESTER, F. 1967. *'Gipsy Moth' Circles The World*. Hodder & Stoughton, London.

CLARK, R. S., HERON, W., FEATHERSTONE, H. M. L., FORGAYS, D. G. and HEBB, D. O. 1951. *Can. J. Psychol.*, **5**, 150–156.

COFOID, D. A. and HONIG, W. K. 1961. *Science*, **134**, 1692–1694.

COLLIAS, N. E. 1952. *Auk*, **69**, 127–159.

COLLIAS, N. E. and COLLIAS, E. C. 1956. *Auk*, **73**, 378–400.

COLLIAS, N. E., COLLIAS, E. C., HUNSAKER, D. and MINNING, L. 1966. *Anim. Behav.*, **14**, 550–559.

COLLIAS, N. E. and JOOS, M. 1953. *Behaviour*, **5**, 175–187.

COLLINS, T. B. 1965. *J. comp. physiol. Psychol.*, **60**, 192–195.

CRAIG, W. 1908. *Am. J. Sociol.*, **14**, 86–100.

CRAIG, W. 1914. *J. Anim. Behav.*, 4, 121–133.

CRAIG, W. 1918. *Biol. Bull.*, **34**, 91–107.

CREW, F. A. E. 1936. *J. Genet.*, **33**, 61–101.

DARWIN, C. R. 1877. *Mind*, **2**, 285–294.

DENENBERG, V. H. 1964. *Psychol. Rev.*, 71, **5**, 335–351.

DENENBERG, V. H. and BELL, R. W. 1960. *Science*, **131**, 227–228.

DENENBERG, V. H. and SMITH, S. A. 1963. *J. comp. physiol. Psychol.*, **56**, 307–312.

DIMOND, S. J. 1965. *Anim. Behav.;* **13**, 101–103.

DIMOND, S. J. 1966. *Anim. Behav.,* **14**, 581.

DOANE, B. K., MAHATOO, W., HERON, W. and SCOTT, T. H. 1959. *Can. J. Psychol.,* **13**, 210–219.

DURFEE, H. and WOLF, K. 1933. *Z. Kinderforsch.,* **42**, 273–320.

EWER, R. F. 1956. *Nature,* **177**, 227–228.

EWER, R. F. 1960. *Behaviour,* **15**, 146–162.

FABRICIUS, E. 1951a. *Acta zool. fenn.,* **68**, 1–175.

FABRICIUS, E. 1951b. *Proc. Xth Int. orn. Congr.,* Uppsala, 1950.

FABRICIUS, E. 1962. *Symp. zool. Soc. Lond.,* **8**, 139–148.

FABRICIUS, E. 1955. *Anim. Behav.,* **3**, 122.

FABRICIUS, E. 1964. *Z. Tierpsychol.,* **21**, 326–337.

FABRICIUS, F. and BOYD, H. 1953. *Wildfowl Trust An. Report,* 1952–53, 84–89.

FISCHER, G. J. 1966. *J. comp. physiol. Psychol.,* **61**, 271–273.

FISCHER, G. J. and CAMPBELL, G. L. 1964. *Anim. Behav.,* **12**, 268–269.

FISCHER, G. J., CAMPBELL, G. L. and DAVIS, W. M. 1965. *J. comp. physiol. Psychol.,* **59**, 455–457.

FISHER, A. E. 1964. In *Proceedings of the First International Symposium on Thirst in the Regulation of Body Water.* Pergamon Press, Oxford.

FISHER, A. E. and HALE, E. B. 1956–57. *Behaviour,* **10**, 309–323.

FORGUS, R. H. 1955. *J. comp. physiol. Psychol.,* **48**, 215–220.

FRISCH, K. VON. 1954. *The Dancing Bees* (translation). Methuen, London.

FRISCH, O. VON. 1957. *Z. Tierpsychol.,* **14**, 231–237.

GADDIS, T. E. 1957. *Birdman of Alcatraz.* Gollancz, London.

GEIST, V. 1963. *Behaviour,* **20**, 377–416.

GEIST, V. 1966. *Behaviour,* **27**, 175–214.

GIBSON, E. J. and WALK, R. D. 1956. *J. comp. physiol. Psychol.,* **49**, 239–242.

GIBSON, E. J., WALK, R. D., PICK, H. L. and TIGHE, T. J. 1958. *J. comp. physiol. Psychol.,* **51**, 584–587.

GIBSON, E. J., WALK, R. D. and TIGHE, T. J. 1959. *J. comp. physiol. Psychol.,* **52**, 74–81.

GIBSON, W. 1953. *The Boat.* Houghton Mifflin, The Riverside Press, Boston.

GLUECK, S. and GLUECK, E. T. 1934. *One Thousand Juvenile Delinquents.* Cambridge, Mass.

GOLDFARB, W. 1943a. *J. Exp. Educ.,* **12**, 106–129.

GOLDFARB, W. 1943b. *Am. J. Orthopsychiat.,* **13**, 249–265.

GOLDFARB, W. 1944a. *Am. J. Orthopsychiat.,* **14**, 162–166.

GOLDFARB, W. 1944b. *Am. J. Orthopsychiat.,* **14**, 441–447.

GOLDFARB, W. 1945. *Am. J. Psychiat.,* **102**, 18–33.

GOODWIN, D. 1948. *Ibis,* **90** 45–48.

GOTTLIEB, G. 1961a. *J. comp. physiol. Psychol.*, **54**, 422–427.

GOTTLIEB, G. 1961b. *Behaviour*, **18**, 205–228.

GOTTLIEB, G. 1963a. *J. comp. physiol. Psychol.*, **56**, 86–91.

GOTTLIEB, G. 1963b. *Anim. Behav.*, **11**, 290–292.

GOTTLIEB, G. 1963c. *Science*, **139**, 497–498.

GOTTLIEB, G. 1963d. *Science*, **140**, 399–400.

GOTTLIEB, G. 1965a. *Science*, **148**, 1596–1598.

GOTTLIEB, G. 1965b. *J. comp. physiol. Psychol.*, **59**, 345–356.

GOTTLIEB, G. 1966. *Anim. Behav.*, **14**, 282–290.

GOTTLIEB, G. 1967. *Abstr. Xth Int. Conf. Ethol.*, Stockholm, 1967.

GOTTLIEB, G. and KLOPFER, P. H. 1962. *J. comp. physiol. Psychol.*, **55**, 821–826.

GOTTLIEB, G. and KUO, Z. Y. 1965, *J. comp. physiol. Psychol.*, **59**, 183–188.

GRABOWSKI, U. 1941. *Z. Tierpsychol.*, **4**, 326–329.

GRAY, P. H. 1958. *J. Psychol.*, **46**, 155–166.

GRAY, P. H. 1960. *Science*, **132**, 1834–1835.

GRAY, P. H. 1961. *J. comp. physiol. Psychol.*, **54**, 597–601.

GRAY, P. H. 1962. *Percept. Mot. Skills*, **14**, 70.

GRAY, P. H. 1964. *Percept. Mot. Skills*, **18**, 445–448.

GRAY, P. H. and HOWARD, K. I. 1957. *Percept. Mot. Skills*, **7**, 301–304.

GRAY, P. H., SALLEE, S. J. and YATES, A. T. 1964. *Percept. Mot. Skills*, **19**, 763–768.

GUHL, A. M. and ORTMAN, L. L. 1953. *Condor*, **55**, 287–297

GUITON, P. 1958. *Proc. phys. Soc. Edinb.*, **27**, 9–14.

GUITON, P. 1959. *Anim. Behav.*, **7**, 26–34.

GUITON, P. 1961. *Anim. Behav.*, **9**, 167–177.

GUITON, P. 1962, *Symp. zool. Soc. Lond.*, **8**, 227–234.

GUITON, P. 1966. *Anim. Behav.*, **14**, 534–538.

GUTEKUNST, R. and YOUNISS, J. 1963. *Percept. Mot. Skills*, **16**, 348.

HAILMAN, J. P. 1959. *Am. Nat.*, **93**, 383–384.

HAILMAN, J. P. and KLOPFER, P. H. 1962. *Anim. Behav.*, **10**, 233–234.

HALDANE, J. B. S. 1954. *Br. J. Anim. Behav.*, **2**, 1.

HARLOW, H. F. and ZIMMERMANN, R. R. 1959. *Science*, **130**, 421–432.

HEBB, D. O. 1949. *The Organisation of Behaviour*. John Wiley, New York.

HEBB, D. O. 1946. *Psychol. Rev.*, **53**, 259–276.

HEINROTH, O. 1911. *Verhandlungen des V. Int. Orn. Kongress*, Berlin, 1901, pp. 587–702.

HEINROTH, O. and HEINROTH, K. 1959. *The Birds* (translation). Faber & Faber, London.

HERSHER, L., RICHMOND, J. B. and MOORE, A. U. 1963. *Behaviour*, **20**, 311–320.

HESS, E. H. 1950. *J. comp. physiol. Psychol.*, **43**, 112–122.

HESS, E. H. 1957. *Ann. N.Y. Acad. Sci.*, **67**, 724–732.

HESS, E. H. 1959a. *J. comp. physiol. Psychol.*, **52**, 515–518.

HESS, E. H. 1959b. *Science*, **130**, 133–141.

HESS, E. H. 1964. *Science*, **146**, 1128–1139.

HESS, E. H. and SCHAEFER, H. H. 1959. *Z. Tierpsychol.*, **16**, 153–160.

HESS, W. R. 1943 (with BRÜGGER, M.), 1944. *Helv. physiol. pharm. Acta.*

HETZER, H. and TUDOR-HART, B. H. 1927. *Quellen und Studien*, **5**, 103–124.

HINDE, R. A. 1955. *Advmt Sci.*, **12**, 19–24.

HINDE, R. A. 1955. *Anim. Behav.*, **3**, 121–122.

HINDE, R. A. 1961. The establishment of the parent offspring relation in birds with some mammalian analogies. In *Current Problems in Animal Behaviour* (W. H. Thorpe and O. L. Zangwill, eds), pp. 175–193.

HINDE, R. A. 1962. *Symp. zool. Soc. Lond.*, **8**, 129–138.

HINDE, R. A. 1962. *Little Club Clin. dev. Med.*, **7**, 25–36.

HINDE, R. A., THORPE, W. H. and VINCE, M. A. 1956. *Behaviour*, **9**, 214–242.

HINKLE, L. E. and WOLFF, H. G. 1956. *A.M.A. Archs. Neurol. Psychiatry*, **76**, 115–174.

HOLST, E. VON and ST PAUL, U. VON. 1963. *Anim. Behav.*, **11**, 1–20.

HUMPHREY, M. and OUNSTED, C. 1963. *Br. J. Psychiat.*, **109**, 599–608.

IGEL, G. J. and CALVIN, A. D. 1960. *J. comp. physiol. Psychol.*, **53**, 302–305.

IMMELMANN, K. 1967. *Abstr. Xth Int. Conf. Ethol.*, Stockholm, 1967.

JAMES, H. 1959. *Can. J. Psychol.*, **13**, 59–67.

JAMES, H. 1960. *Anim. Behav.*, **8**, 223–224.

JAMES, H. 1962. *Anim. Behav.*, **10**, 341–346.

JAMES, H. and BINKS, C. 1963. *Science*, **139**, 1293–1294.

JAMES, WM. 1890. *Principles of Psychology*, 2 vols. Holt, New York.

JAYNES, J. 1956. *J. comp. physiol. Psychol.*, **49**, 201–206.

JAYNES, J. 1957. *J. comp. physiol. Psychol.*, **50**, 6–10.

JAYNES, J. 1958a. *J. comp. physiol. Psychol.*, **51**, 234–237.

JAYNES, J. 1958b. *J. comp. physiol. Psychol.*, **51**, 238–242.

JOHNSGARD, P. A. 1960. *Ibis*, **102**, 616–618.

JOHNSGARD, P. A. 1965. *Handbook of Waterfowl Behaviour*. Constable, London.

KAILA, E. 1932. *Annls Univ. fenn. åbo.*, **17**, 1–114.

KAUFMAN, I. C. and HINDE, R. A. 1961. *Anim. Behav.*, **9**, 197–204.

KEAR, J. 1960. *Ibis*, **102**, 614–616

KLINGHAMMER, E. and HESS, E. H. 1964. *Science*, **146**, 265–266.

KLOPFER, P. H. 1956, *Wilson Bull.*, **68**, 320–321.

KLOPFER, P. H. 1957. *Am. Nat.*, **91**, 856, 61–63.

KLOPFER, P. H. 1958. *Science*, **128**, 903.

KLOPFER, P. H. 1959a. *Wilson Bull.*, **71**, 262–266.

KLOPFER, P. H. 1959b. *Ecology*, **40**, 90–102.

KLOPFER, P. H. 1959c. *Behaviour*, **14**, 282–299.

KLOPFER, P. H. 1961. *Behaviour*, **17**, 71–79.

KLOPFER, P. H. 1964. *Am. Nat.*, **98**, 900, 173–182.

KLOPFER, P. H. 1965a. *Science*, **147**, 302–303.

KLOPFER, P. H. 1965b. *Wilson Bull.*, **77**, 376–381.

KLOPFER, P. H. 1967a. *Behavl Sci.*, **12**, 122–129.

KLOPFER, P. H. 1967b. *Abstr. Xth Int. Conf. Ethol.*, Stockholm, 1967.

KLOPFER, P. H., ADAMS, D. K. and KLOPFER, M. S. 1964. *Proc. natn. Acad. Sci. U.S.A.*, **52**, 911–914.

KLOPFER, P. H. and GAMBLE, J. 1966. *Z. Tierpsychol.*, **23**, 588–592.

KLOPFER, P. H. and GOTTLIEB, G. 1962a. *Z. Tierpsychol.*, **19**, 183–190.

KLOPFER, P. H. and GOTTLIEB, G. 1962b. *J. comp. physiol Psychol.*, **55**, 126–130.

KLOPFER, P. H. and HAILMAN, J. P. 1964a. *Z. Tierpsychol.*, **21**, 755–762.

KLOPFER, P. H. and HAILMAN, J. P. 1964b. *Science*, **145**, 1333–1334.

KOVACH, J. K. 1964. *J. comp. physiol. Psychol.*, **57**, 183–187.

KOVACH, J. K. and HESS, E. H. 1963. *J. comp. physiol. Psychol.*, **56**, 461–464.

KOVACH, J. K., FABRICIUS, E. and FÄLT, L. 1966. *J. comp. physiol. Psychol.*, **61**, 449–454.

KRUIJT, J. P. *Symp. zool. Soc. Lond.*, **8**, 219–226.

KRUIJT, J. P. 1964. *Behaviour*, Supp. 12.

KUO, Z. Y. 1932. *J. comp. Psychol.*, **14**, 109–121.

LACK, D. 1953. *The Life of the Robin*. Pelican Books, London.

LANDSBOROUGH THOMPSON, A. 1964. *A New Dictionary of Birds*. Nelson, London.

LASHLEY, K. S. 1929. *Brain Mechanisms and Intelligence*, Univ. Chicago Press.

LASHLEY, K. S. 1938. *Psychol. Rev.*, **45**, 445–471.

LEAGUE OF NATIONS. 1938. *Prostitutes: Their Early Lives*. Geneva.

LEHRMAN, D. S. 1953. *Q, Rev. Biol.*, **28**, 337–363.

LEVINE, S. 1962. *Little Club Clin. dev. Med.*, **7**, 18–24.

LEVINE, S. and LEWIS, G. W. 1959a. *J. comp. physiol. Psychol.*, **52**, 368–369.

LEVINE, S. and LEWIS, G. W. 1959b. *Science*, **129**, 42–43.

LEVINE, S. and OTIS, L. S. 1958. *Can. J. Psychol.*, **12**, 103–108.

LEVY, D. M. 1934. *Am. J. Orthopsychiat.*, **4**, 203–274.

LEVY, D. M. 1938. *J. genet. Psychol.*, **18**, 327–348.

LEVY, D. M. 1944. *Am. J. Orthopsychiat.*, **14**, 644–671.

LEWIS, M. 1964. *J. comp. physiol. Psychol.*, **57**, 367–372.

LIDDELL, H. 1960. In *Stress and Psychiatric Disorder. Experimental Neurosis in Animals* (J. M. Tanner, ed.). Blackwell, Oxford.

LIFTON, R. J. 1956. *Psychiatry*, **19**, 173–195.

LILL, A. and WOOD-GUSH, D. G. M. 1965. *Behaviour*, **25**, 16–44.

LILLY, J. C. 1956. *Psychiat. Res. Rep.* No. 5, 1–28.

LINDAUER, M. 1961. *Communication Among Social Bees*, Harvard Univ. Press.

LORENZ, K. Z. 1935. *J. Orn.*, **83**, 137–213. 289–413.

LORENZ, K. Z. 1937. *Auk*, **54**, 245–273.

LORENZ, K. Z. 1941. *J. Orn.*, **89** (supp.), 194–294.

LORENZ, K. Z. 1950. *Symp. Soc. exp. Biol.*, W. 221–268.

LORENZ, K. Z. 1952. *King Solomon's Ring*. Methuen, London.

LORENZ, K. Z. 1955. In *Group Processes* (B. Schaffner, ed.), pp. 168–220. Josiah Macey Foundation, New York.

LORENZ, K. Z. 1957, In *The Nature of Instinct* (C. H. Schiller, ed.). Int. Univ. Press, New York.

LORENZ, K. Z. 1966. The evolution of behaviour. *Psychobiology*, pp. 33–42. W. H. Freeman, San Francisco. (Reprint from *Scient. Am.*, 1958.)

LORENZ, K. Z. 1960. *Fortschr. Zool.*, **12**, 263–294.

LORENZ, K. Z. 1966. *On Aggression*. Methuen, London.

MCBRIDE, G. 1963. *Anim. Behav.*, **11**, 53–56.

MCBRIDE, G. 1964. *Anim. Behav.*, **12**, 264–267.

MCBRIDE, G. 1967. *Abstr. Xth Int. Conf. Ethol.*, Stockholm, 1967.

MCDOUGALL, WM. 1936. *Introduction to Social Psychology*, 23rd edn. Methuen, London.

MARKS, H. L., SIEGEL, P. B. and KRAMER, C. Y. 1960. *Anim. Behav.*, **8**, 192–196.

MARLER, P. 1956. *Ibis*, **98**, 231–261.

MARLER, P. 1961. In *Current Problems in Animal Behaviour* (W. H. Thorpe and O. L. Zangwill, eds.), pp. 150–166. Cambridge Univ. Press.

MARR, J. N. 1964. *J. genet. Psychol.*, **104**, 35–64.

MATTHEWS, W. A. and HEMMINGS, G. 1963. *Nature*, **198**, 1183–1184.

MATURANA, H. R., LETTVIN, J. Y., MCCULLOUGH and PITTS, W. H. 1960. *J. genet. Physiol.*, **46**, 129.

MATURANA, H. R. and FRENK, S. 1963. *Science*, **142**, 977–979.

MELZACK, R. and THOMPSON, W. R. 1956. *Can. J. Psychol.*, **10**, 82–90.

MENNER, E. 1938. *Zool. Jb. Abt. allg. Zool. Physiol.*, **48**, 481–583.

MENUT, G. 1943. *La dissociation familiale et les troubles du caractère chez l'enfant*. Paris.

MEYERS, N. J. 1962. *J. comp. physiol. Psychol.*, **55**, 1099–1101.

MILLS, T. W. 1896. *The Nature and Development of Animal Intelligence*. Macmillan, New York.

MOLTZ, H. 1960. *Psychol. Bull.*, **57**, 291–314.

MOLTZ, H. 1963. *Psychol. Rev.*, **70**, 123–138.

MOLTZ, H. and ROSENBLUM, L. A. 1958a. *J. comp. physiol. Psychol.*, **57**, 580–583.

MOLTZ, H. and ROSENBLUM, L. A. 1958b. *J. comp. physiol. Psychol.*, **51**, 658–661.

MOLTZ, H., ROSENBLUM, L. and HALIKAS, N. 1959. *J. comp. physiol. Psychol.* **52**, 240–241.

MOLTZ, H., ROSENBLUM, L. and STETTNER, J. 1960. *J. comp. physiol. Psychol.*, **53**, 297–301.

MOLTZ, H. and STETTNER, L. J. 1961. *J. comp. physiol. Psychol.*, **54**, 279–283.

MOLTZ, H. and STETTNER, L. J. 1962. *J. comp. physiol. Psychol.*, **55**, 626–632.

NICE, M. M. 1953. *Condor*, **55**, 33–37.

NICOLAI, J. 1956. *Z. Tierpsychol.*, **13**, 93–132.

NISSEN, H. W., CHOW, K. L. and SEMMES, J. 1951. *Am. J. Psychol.*, **64**, 485–507.

NOBLE, G. K. and CURTIS, B. 1935–36. *Anat. Rec.* **64**, 84–85.

NOBLE, G. K. and CURTIS, B. 1939. *Bull. N.Y. St. Mus.* (*Nat. Hist.*), **76**, 1–46.

NOTTEBOHM, F. 1967. *Abstr. Xth Int. Conf. Ethol.*, Stockholm, 1967.

PADILLA, S. G. 1935. *J. comp. Psychol.*, **20**, 413–443.

PAULSEN, G. W. 1965. *Exp. Neurol.*, **11**, 324–333.

PETERS, J. J., CUSICK, C. J. and VONDERAHE, A. R. 1963. *Am. J. Physiol.*, **204**, 304–308.

PETERS, J. J. and ISAACSON, R. L. 1963. *J. comp. physiol. Psychol.*, **56**, 793–796.

PETERS, J. J. VONDERAHE, A. R. and POWERS, T. H. 1958. *J. exp. Zool.*, **139**, 459–468.

PETERSON, N. 1960. *Science*, **132**, 1395–1396.

PHILLIPS, R. E. and SIEGEL, P. B. 1966. *Anim. Behav.*, **14**, 84–88.

PITZ, G. F. and ROSS, R. B. 1961. *J. comp. physiol. Psychol.*, **54**, 602–604.

PLINY. *Natural History*, Book X.51. [Pliny also cited by Thorpe (1963).]

POLT, J. M. and HESS, E. H. 1964. *Science*, **143**, 1185–1187.

POLT, J. M. and HESS, E. H. 1966. *J. comp. physiol. Psychol.*, **61**, 268–270.

PRUGH, D. G., STAUB, E. M. and SANDS, H. H. 1953. *Am J.. Orthopsychiat.*, **23**, 70–106.

PUMPHREY, R. J. 1948. *Ibis*, **90**, 171–199.

RÄBER, H. 1948. *Behaviour*, **1**, 237–266.

RAMSAY, A. U. 1951. *Auk*, **68**, 1–16.

RAMSAY, A. O. and HESS, E. H. 1954. *Wilson Bull.*, **66**, 196–206.

RATNER, S. C. and THOMPSON, R. W. 1960. *Anim. Behav.*, **8**, 186–191.

RIBBLE, M. A. 1943. *The Rights of Infants*, Columbia Univ. Press, New York.

RICE, C. F. 1962. *Science*, **138**, 680–681.

RIESEN, A. H. 1950. *Scient. Am.*, **183**, 16–19.

RITTER, C. 1954. *A Woman in the Polar Night*. Allen & Unwin, London.

SACKETT, G. P. 1963. *Psychol. Rev.*, **70**, 40–50.

SALZEN, E. A. 1962. *Symp. zool. Soc. Lond.*, **8**, 199–217.

SALZEN, E. A. 1963a. *Anim. Behav.*, **11**, 66–71.

SALZEN, E. A. 1963b. *J. Genet. Psychol.*, **102**, 51–54.

SALZEN, E. A. 1966. *Behaviour*, **26**, 286–322.

SALZEN, E. A. and SLUCKIN, W. 1959. *Anim. Behav.*, **7**, 172–179.

SALZEN, E. A. and TOMLIN, F. J. 1963. *Anim. Behav.*, **11**, 62–65.

SCHAEFER, H. H. and HESS, E. H. 1959. *Z. Tierpsychol.*, **16**, 153–160.

SCHAFFER, H. R. 1958. *Brit. J. med. Psychol.*, **31**, 174–183.

SCHAFFER, H. R. and EMERSON, P. 1964. *Monogr. Soc. Res. Child Dev.* **94**, 29, 3.

SCHALLER, G. B. and EMLEN, J. T. 1962. *Anim. Behav.*, **10**, 370–381.

SCHEIN, E. H. 1956. *Psychiatry*, **19**, 149–172.

SCHEIN, M. W. 1963. *Z. Tierpsychol.*, **20**, 462–467.

SCHEIN, M. W., FITCH, R. J. and HART, F. M. 1962. *Am. Zool.*, **2**, 21.

SCHEIN, M. W. and HALE, E. B. 1959. *Anim. Behav.*, **7**, 189–200.

SCHNEIRLA, T. C. 1952. *Psychol. Bull.*, **149**, 559–597.

SCHNEIRLA, T. C. and ROSENBLATT, J. S. 1963. *Science*, **139**, 1110–1115.

SCHUTZ, F. 1963a. *Naturwissenchaften*, **19**, 624–625.

SCHUTZ, F. 1963b. *Verh. dr. zool. Ges..*, **27**, 282–287.

SCHUTZ, F. 1964. *Z. exp. angew. Psychol.*, **11**, 169–178.

SCHUTZ, F. 1965a. *Z. Tierpsychol.*, **22**, 50–103.

SCHUTZ, F. 1965b. *Psychol. Forsch.*, **28**, 439–463.

SCHUTZ, F. 1966. *Stud. Gen.*, **19**, 273–285.

SCHWARTZKOPF, J. 1955. *Auk*, **72**, 340–347.

SCOTT, J. P. 1962. *Science*, **138**, 949–958.

SCOTT, J. P. and MARSTON, M. 1950. *J. genet. Psychol.*, **77**, 25–60.

SCOTT, T. H., BEXTON, W. H., HERON, W. and DOANE, B. K. 1959. *Can. J. Pyschol.*, **13**, 200–209.

SHIPLEY, W. U. 1963. *Anim. Behav.*, **11**, 470–474.

SIEGEL, H. S. and SIEGEL, P. B. 1961. *Anim. Behav.*, **9**, 151–158.

SIEGEL, P. B. and SIEGEL, H. S. 1964. *Anim. Behav.*, **12**, 270–271.

SIMNER, M. L. 1966. *J. comp. physiol. Psychol.*, **61**, 496–498.

SKEELS, H. M. and HARMS, I. J. 1948. *J. Genet. Psychol.*, **72**, 283.

SLADEN, W. J. L. 1958. *Falkland Islands Dependencies Survey*, **17**.

SLOCUM, J. 1963. *Sailing Alone Around the World*. Hart-Davis, London.

SLUCKIN, W. 1962. *Symp. zool. Soc. Lond.*, **8**, 193–198.

SLUCKIN, W. and SALZEN, E. A. 1961. *J. exp. Psychol.*, **13**, 65–77.

SMITH, F. V. 1960. *Anim. Behav.*, **8**, 197–200.

SMITH, F. V. 1962. *Symp. zool. Soc. Lond.*, **8**, 171–191.

SMITH, F. V. 1965. *Anim. Behav.*, **13**, 84–86.

SMITH, F. V. and BIRD, M. W. 1963a. *Anim. Behav.*, **11**, 57–61.

SMITH, F. V. and BIRD, M. W. 1963b. *Anim. Behav.*, **11**, 300–305.

SMITH, F. V. and BIRD, M. W. 1963c. *Anim. Behav.*, **11**, 397–399.

SMITH, F. V. and BIRD, M. W. 1964a. *Anim. Behav.*, **12**, 60–63.

SMITH, F. V. and BIRD, M. W. 1964b. *Anim. Behav.*, **12**, 252–258.

SMITH, F. V. and BIRD, M. W. 1964c. *Anim. Behav.*, **12**, 259–263.

SMITH, F. V. and HOYES, P. A. 1961. *Anim. Behav.*, **9**, 159–166.

SMITH, F. V. and TEMPLETON, W. B. 1966. *Anim. Behav.*, **14**, 291–295.

SMITH, F. V., VAN-TOLLER, C. and BOYES, T. 1966. *Anim. Behav.*, **14**, 120–125.

SMITH, F. V. and HARDING, L. W. (unpublished) The effect of a conventional reinforcer on the imprinting-type response.

SMITH, F. V. and NOTT, K. (in press) The critical period in relation to the strength of the stimulus.

SMITH, W. 1957. *Behaviour*, **11**, 40–53.

SPALDING, D. 1954. *Br. J. Anim. Behav.*, **2**, 2–11.

SPITZ, R. A. 1946a. *Genet. Psychol. Mongr.*, **34**, 57–125.

SPITZ, R. A. 1946b. *Psychoanal. Study Child*, **2**, 313–342.

SPITZ, R. and WOLF, K. 1945. *Psychoanal. Study Child*, **1**, 53–74.

STEVEN, D. M. 1955. *Br. J. Anim. Behav.*, **1**, 14–16.

STOTT, D. H. 1950. *Delinquency and Human Nature*. Dunfermline.

SWANBERG, P. O. 1951. *Proc. Xth Int. orn. Congr.*, Uppsala, 1950, pp. 545–554.

TAYLOR, A., SLUCKIN, W., HEWITT, R. and GUITON, P. 1967. *Anim. Behav.*, **15**, 514–519.

TAYLOR, A. and TAYLOR, K. F. 1964. *Nature*, **204**, 1117–1118.

TAYLOR, K. F. and SLUCKIN, W. 1964. *Nature*, **201**, 108–109.

THOMPSON, W. R. and DUBANOSKI, R. A. 1964. *Anim. Behav.*, **12**, 213–218.

THOMPSON, W. R. and DUBANOSKI, R. A. 1964, *Science*, **143**, 1187–1188.

THOMPSON, W. R. and HERON, W. 1954. *Can. J. Psychol.*, **8**, 17–51.

THORPE, W. H. 1961. Sensitive periods in the learning of animals and men. Chap. 8 in *Current Problems in Animal Behaviour* (W. H. Thorpe and O. L. Zangwill, eds). Cambridge Univ. Press.

THORPE, W. H. 1963. *Learning and Instinct in Animals*, 2nd edn. Methuen, London.

TIIRA, E. 1954. *Raft of Despair*. Hutchinson, London.

TINBERGEN, N. 1951. *The Study of Instinct.* Oxford Univ. Press.

TINBERGEN, N. 1959. *Behaviour*, **15**, 1–70.

TINBERGEN, N., BROEKHUYSEN, G. J., FEEKES, F., HOUGHTON, J. C. W., KRUUK, H. and SZULC, E. 1962. *Behaviour*, **19**, 74–117.

TOLMAN, C. W. 1967. *Anim. Behav.*, **15**, 145–148.

TOLMAN, C. W. and WILSON, C. W. 1965. *Anim. Behav.*, **13**, 134–142.

TURNER, E. R. A. 1965. *Behaviour*, **24**, 1–46.

UEXKÜLL, J. VON. 1921. *Umwelt und Innenwelt der Tiere*, 2nd edn. Berlin.

VINCE, M. A. 1958. *Anim. Behav.*, **6**, 53–59.

VINCE, M. A. 1960. *Behaviour*, **15**, 219–243.

VINCE, M. A. 1964. *Anim. Behav.*, **12**, 531–534.

VINCE, M. A. 1966a. *Anim. Behav.*, **14**, 34–40.

VINCE, M. A. 1966b. *Anim. Behav.*, **14**, 389–394.

WALK, R. D., GIBSON, E. J., PICK, H. L. and TIGHE, T. J. 1958. *J. comp. physiol. Psychol.*, **51**, 483–487.

WALK, R. D., GIBSON, E. J., PICK, H. L. and TIGHE, T. J. 1959. *J. comp. physiol. Psychol.*, **52**, 519–521.

WALLER, P. F. and WALLER, M. B. 1963. *Behaviour*, **20**, 343–363.

WARRINER, C. C., LEMMON, W. B. and RAY, T. S. 1963. *Anim. Behav.*, **11**, 221–224.

WATSON, J. B. 1908. *Pap. Tortugas Lab.*, **2**, 187–255.

WATT, G. 1951. *The Farne Islands: Their History and Wild Life.* London.

WEIDMANN, U. 1956a. *Anim. Behav.*, **4**, 78–79.

WEIDMANN, U. 1956b. *Z. Tierpsychol.*, **13**, 208–271.

WEIDMANN, U. 1958. *Z. Tierpsychol.*, **15**, 277–300.

WERNER, H. 1940. *The Comparative Psychology of Mental Development.* Harper, New York.

WEXLER, D., MENDELSON, J., LEIDERMAN, H. and SOLOMON, P. 1958. *Archs Neurol. Psychiat.*, **79**, 225–233.

WHITMAN, C. O. 1898. *Biol. Lect. mar. biol. Lab., Wood's Hole.* Publ. Boston, 1899, pp. 285–338.

WHITMAN, C. O. 1919. *Orthogenic Evolution in Pigeons. Vol. 3: The Behaviour of Pigeons* (Harvey Carr, ed.). Carnegie Inst., Washington; Publication 257.

WOOD-GUSH, D. G. M. 1954. *Br. J. Anim. Behav.*, **2**, 95–102.

WOOD-GUSH, D. G. M. 1955. *Anim. Behav.*, **3**, 81–110.

WOOD-GUSH, D. G. M. 1956. *Anim. Behav.*, **4**, 133–142.

WOOD-GUSH, D. G. M. 1957. *Anim. Behav.*, **5**, 1–5.

WOOD-GUSH, D. G. M. 1958. *Anim. Behav.*, **6**, 68–71.

WÜRDIGER, I. 1967. *Abstr. Xth. Int. Conf. Ethol.*, Stockholm, 1967.

Index of First Authors

General Index

(Scientific names of animals are given in the text)